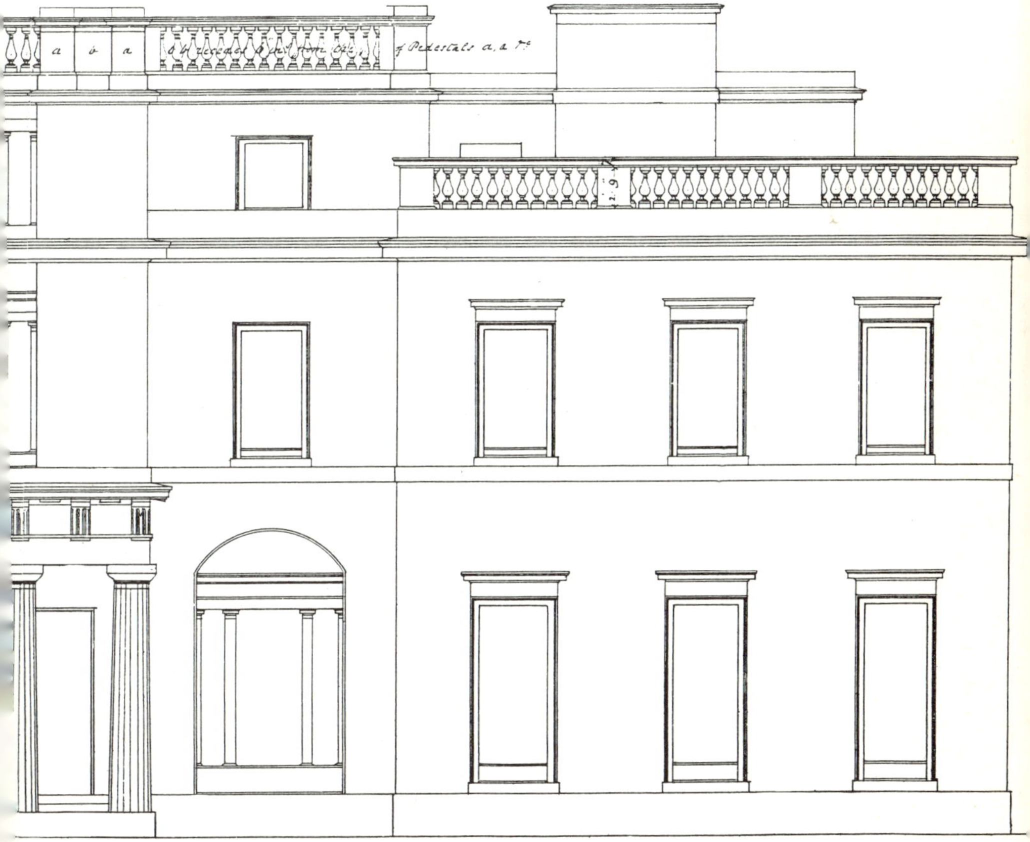
a
b
a
of Pedestals a, a &c

LIFE IN A SCOTTISH COUNTRY HOUSE

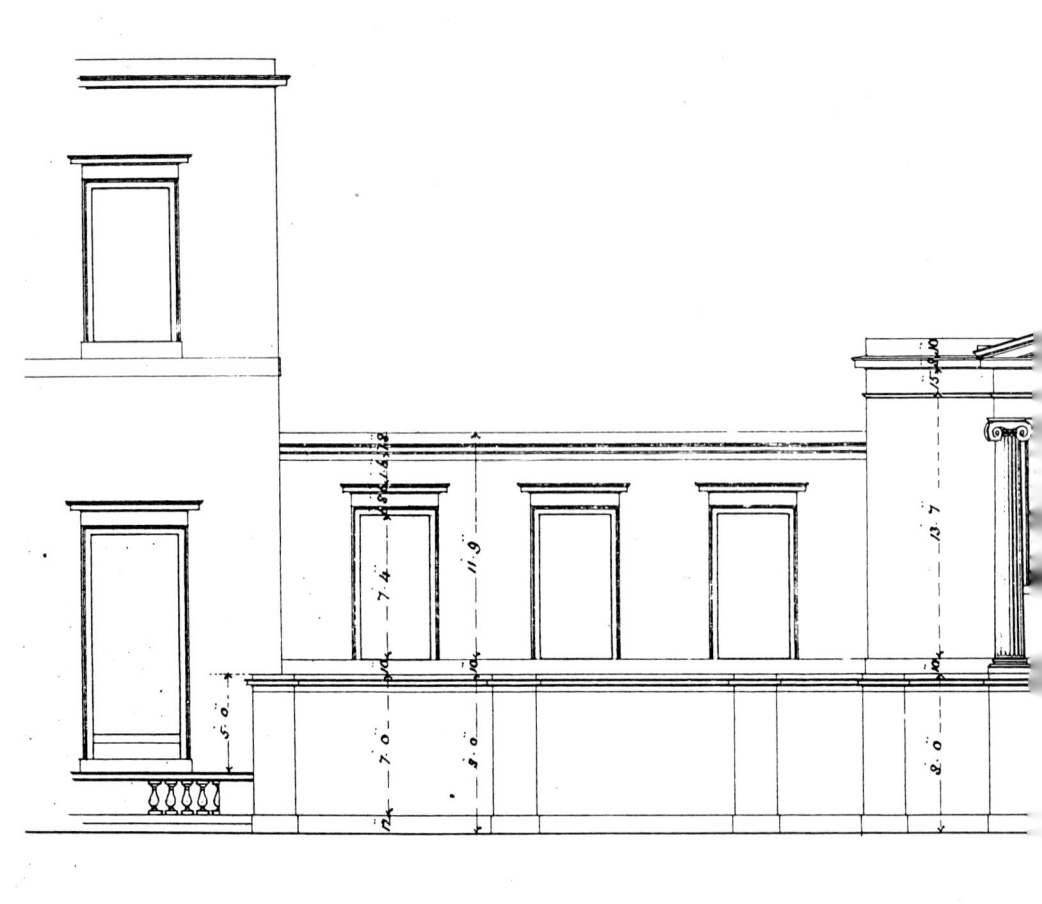

Jan. 30. 1827 N. 13. The front wall above will be raised to
13.6 in place of 11.9 as marked &
the additional height added to the room —

LIFE IN A SCOTTISH COUNTRY HOUSE
The Story of A J Balfour and Whittingehame House

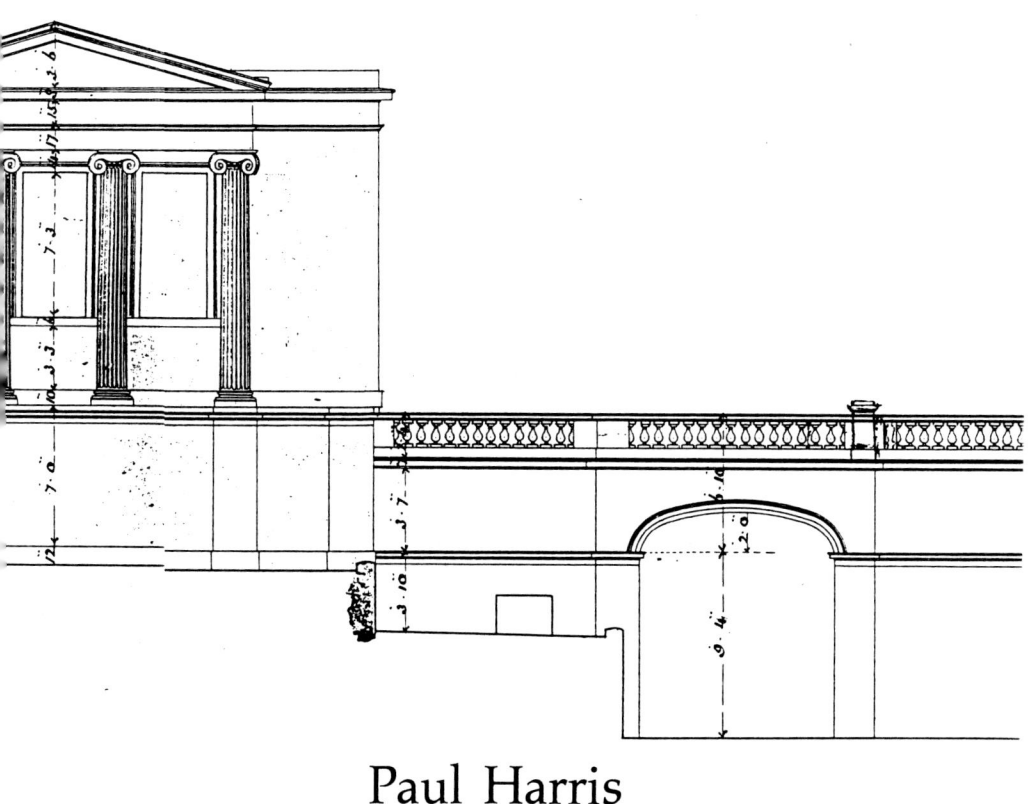

Paul Harris

Whittingehame House Publishing

First published 1989 by
Whittingehame House Publishing
Whittingehame House
Whittingehame
Haddington EH41 4QA
© copyright Paul Harris 1989
Produced in a limited edition of which 750 copies are for sale

> **British Library Cataloguing in Publication Data**
>
> Harris, Paul, 1948-
> Life in a scottish country house: the story
> of A. J. Balfour and Whittingehame House.
> 1. Lothian (region). Whittingehame. Country
> houses.
> Whittingehame house
> I. Title
> 941.3'6
>
> ISBN 0-9514985-0-9

Other books by Paul Harris

A Concise Dictionary of Scottish Painters
Investing in Scottish Pictures
Edinburgh Since 1900   Aberdeen Since 1900
Aberdeen at War
Glasgow at War
Tyneside at War (with Clive Hardy)
Edinburgh: The Fabulous Fifties
By Appointment: The Story of Balmoral and Royal Deeside
When Pirates Ruled the Waves
To Be a Pirate King
Broadcasting from the High Seas
The Garvie Trial
Oil
The Little Scots Cookbook
Cooking with Beer
The Best of Bangladesh (with Tommy Miah)
Scotland: An Anthology (Ed.)
Disaster !

Text typeset in 10 pt. Palatino from disc supplied
by Paul Harris Editorial Consultancy

Printed and bound by Gorenjski Tisk Printing Company,
Kranj, Yugoslavia

CONTENTS

Acknowledgements 7

List of Illustrations 8

Prologue 11

"A truly palatial appearance" 15

"An event of no small importance..." 39

"A whirlpool of everything in life" 51

"Disappointment when you are dealing with builders" 71

"I am uneasy about my affairs" 95

"Less adaptable..." 109

Epilogue 119

References 127

Bibliography 129

Chronology 131

Genealogy 132

Proprietors 135

Glossary of Domestic & Architectural Terms 135

Index 137

Appendix One 141

Appendix Two 142

1 Arthur James Balfour: statesman, philosopher and head of the household at Whittingehame.

ACKNOWLEDGEMENTS

My thanks go particularly to Lord Balfour for his assistance with my researches and for making family documents and diaries available to me on an unrestricted basis. I am grateful to all those who read the manuscript of this little book and gave me the benefit of their comments, especially Charles Skilton and Neil Cameron, and also those, too numerous to mention, who were so generous with their recollections. It has sometimes been difficult to identify accurately the sequence of events and where oral evidence has conflicted with written material, the latter has ruled. The responsibility for any mistakes is, of course, entirely my own.

Illustrations 7, 8, 10, 11, 13 & 14, Smirke's drawings and plans, are reproduced courtesy of the Royal Institute of British Architects Drawings Collection; illustrations 21 & 22, William Burn's elevations, are reproduced courtesy of The Royal Commission on the Ancient and Historical Monuments of Scotland in Edinburgh; photograph 63 is reproduced courtesy of The Scotsman Publications Ltd.; number 19 courtesy of Mr & Mrs Harrower; number 57 courtesy Lawrence Read; numbers 17 & 58 courtesy Michael Clarkson; number 39 courtesy the Fine Art Society Ltd.; I am grateful to the Keeper of the Records of Scotland, Edinburgh, and to Lord Balfour for permission to reproduce pictures numbered 23, 28, 31, 34, 35, 38, 41, 42, 43, 44, 48, and 51. Other photographs are my own.

Paul Harris

Whittingehame House

July 1989

ILLUSTRATIONS

Endpapers: Elevation of the entrance front by William Burn (1827). *Title pages*: Elevation of the west wing by William Burn (1827).

1. Arthur James Balfour: statesman, philosopher and head of the household at Whittingehame.
2. Whittingehame House, the south front, 1986.
3. Lady Frances Balfour by Sir Edward Burne-Jones: astute observer and prolific correspondent.
4. Blanche Balfour, daughter of Lady Frances and Eustace Balfour, by Sir Edward Burne-Jones: writer and biographer of A J Balfour.
5. James Balfour, grandfather of A J Balfour, who ordered the House built in 1817.
6. Sir Robert Smirke, architect of Whittingehame House. Bust by Thomas Campbell, 1845.
7. Perspective of The Entrance Front, inscr. Albany Decr 4th 1817. An artist's impression in watercolour prepared for the client in Smirke's London office.
8. Perspective of The South Front, inscr. Albany Decr 4th 1817.
9. Aerial view of Whittingehame House, entrance front from the north.
10. Plan of the Principal Story, by Smirke, 1817.
11. Plan of the Chamber Story, by Smirke, 1817.
12. Aerial view of Whittingehame House, south facade.
13. Plan of the Attic Story, by Smirke, 1817.
14. Plan of the Basement Story, by Smirke, 1817.
15. The West lodge, by Smirke (1818).
16. The East lodge, by Smirke (1818).
17. Aerial view of the Stable block, by Smirke (1818).
18. Whittingehame Tower from the south east, postcard view *circa* 1905.
19. The later Half Moon Lodge (demolished 1964).
20. William Burn's extension for domestic offices, 1827.
21. Elevation of the west wing by William Burn (1827).
22. William Burn's elevation of the entrance front incorporating his changes (1827).
23. Whittingehame House, north entrance front, photograph *circa* 1870. Note the *porte cochere* which allows carriages to draw up under cover. This was infilled, 1901.
24. James Maitland Balfour, father of A J Balfour, painted at the age of 17 by George Richmond.
25. Lady Blanche Balfour, mother of A J Balfour, painted at the age of 22 by James R Swinton.

26 Lady Blanche and her family at the front of the house, *circa* 1866.
27 The magic lantern show: a Victorian engraving of a popular activity at Whittingehame.
28 The cover of *The Whittinghame Advertiser*, 1867.
29 A J Balfour's uncle, Robert Cecil, 3rd Marquess of Salisbury (by Phil May).
30 A Victorian view of leisured life on the croquet lawn.
31 Croquet on the lower lawn, *circa* 1869-70. Note the conservatory, demolished in the renovations of 1871.
32 Visitor to Whittingehame, W E Gladstone, Prime Minister and leader of the Liberal Party (by Phil May).
33 Joseph Chamberlain and A J Balfour caricatured in *Punch* (1903).
34 Day trip to the beach near Tyninghame: Alison, Joan, Nellie, Ruth and Gerald, 1906.
35 Mrs Helen Anderson, housekeeper from 1875, taken in 1903.
36 The main hall with its Saucer-domed ceiling.
37 The terrace created on A J Balfour's instructions, 1872.
38 The dining room prior to the remodelling of 1899. An arts and craft style side table had already appeared.
39 The ornate arts and crafts style overmantel by Alexander Fisher (1900) installed in the renovated dining room.
40 The richly moulded dining room ceiling by Eustace Balfour and Lawrence Turner (1899).
41 Family and guests at the door of the House, September 1902.
42 The Upper Library, November 1904.
43 A J Balfour's study at Whittingehame, 1919.
44 The Library in 1919. A photograph taken for *The Scots Pictorial*
45 A J Balfour on the links at North Berwick.
46 A cartoon satirising Balfour's preoccupations with golf and motoring.
47 The De Dion motor car in front of the house, 1900, with Blanche Balfour at the wheel.
48 The 40 h.p. Napier in front of the House with A J Balfour and Mills, the driver, in the front, behind Alison, Joan, Nellie and Ruth.
49 A J Balfour, as Prime Minister, pictured by *Punch* in one sporting activity in which he did not participate!
50 A J Balfour starting for a motor ride.
51 The village of Whittingehame in the snow, 1902.
52 The arts and crafts movement, patronised so enthusiastically by Arthur and Eustace Balfour from its earl-

iest days, was the butt of much satirical comment, as in this *Punch* cartoon.
53 The Balfour Declaration, drafted at Whittingehame, August 1917.
54 First notes by Balfour for for his autobiography, made at Whittingehame, 1928.
55 The Earl of Balfour with his great-nephew Gerald (4th Earl) on the terrace at Whittingehame, 1928.
56 The main staircase after the House was vacated.
57 Holt School Young Farmers' Club.
58 Holt School for Boys. The last year, 1979-80, photographed on the south terrace.
59 Vandalism in the empty library (1986).
60 Restoration work at the House, 1987.
61 Extensive removal of damaged plaster was required.
62 New classical pillars in the former nursery, January 1987.
63 Paul & Carol Ann Harris in the same room, May 1989.
64 Restoration work in the library. Graffiti and white paint are removed from the scagliola pillars.
65 Door handle designed by Sir Robert Lorimer (1901).
66 Installation of modern plumbing (1986).
67 The roof of lead with slated sections and two cupolas, over the main stair and the nursery stair.
68 Life returns to the lawns, June 1989.
69 Holograph dedication by A J Balfour to Lady Frances Balfour on the flyleaf of *Alfred Lord Tennyson: A Memoir by His Son*.
70 On the terrace: refugees from the 19th century.
71 The *Punch* view of the shaky Balfour administration 1902-5.
72 Whittingehame House from the south west, 1987.

PROLOGUE

It might appear the height of self indulgence to attempt to write a book on the house in which you live, particularly for a writer who must, perforce, live from his writing, but the story of Whittingehame House is no ordinary tale of some mass of masonry inhabited by succeeding generations of nondescripts. It is not only the story of an architecturally important building, constructed by one of the leading architects of the day, but it also encompasses the story of one of the most interesting and influential families in this country during the late 19th and early 20th century.

But first a note about the genesis of this book. There appeared in April 1986 in the Property Section of *The Scotsman* an unusually modest advertisement in the classified section which seemed in inverse proportion to the scale of the property advertised.

WHITTINGEHAME HOUSE

> Mansion House and Policies. The former home of the Earl of Balfour situated in its own grounds with woodland, tennis court and fishing rights. Accommodation comprises entrance hall, reception hall, 3 lounges, dining hall, 2 drawing rooms, 2 libraries, livingroom, study, office, 33 bedrooms, 2 kitchens, 8 bathrooms, cloakrooms, storage.

> Offers are invited in the region of £120,000

I must confess I was at that time only vaguely aware of the location of Whittingehame somewhere in deepest East Lothian and I supposed that it really must be rather off the beaten track with an asking price that worked out at around £2,000 per room, not to mention tennis courts, policies, fishing and historical connections with A J Balfour, the Prime Minister. I was intrigued, to put it mildly, and not least because I had just been asked to find a country house within striking distance of Edinburgh by a publisher client in the south of England, Charles Skilton.

Lacking anything more illuminating than a small scale Road Atlas of Great Britain, actually finding Whittingehame, which was not marked, was a minor achievement. Although I did not realise it at the time, perhaps therein lay the explanation for the preservation of the property, hidden in its secret fold beneath the Lammermuir Hills, which rise to the south beyond the fertile farming land of East Lothian. But that is to jump ahead.

The first sight of the House, approached by a narrow, gently climbing drive which passed the former stables, was, quite literally, breathtaking. The first impression was one of a vast bulk of masonry, massive in effect. After a few seconds the scale and classical symmetry became apparent. From the outside, at least, the condition of the building appeared to be sound. Inside, there was evidence of a range of problems, largely arising from many years of institutional use and general neglect. The overpowering impression of the place was of its enormous size. The rooms and the corridors just seemed to go on and on endlessly . . . On that first visit it took more than two hours just to walk around the house, without undertaking any sort of detailed inspection. Including the enormous rambling basement and later extensions, we counted 86 rooms. Despite its vastness, its institutional green, the hardboard nailed to the walls, the water flowing through cracked and collapsed ceilings and the general air of abandonment which lay heavy in the rooms and corridors, we were excited by the atmosphere and potential for living in the building.

Hardly unexpectedly, the House was besieged by hopeful bargain hunters but most turned away disappointed. The sheer physical size of the undertaking was daunting. It was clearly too vast for a private residence for even the wealthiest and most ostentatious. It would

2 Whittingehame House, the south front, 1986.

3 *Above*: Lady Frances Balfour by Sir Edward Burne-Jones: astute observer and prolific correspondent.

4 *Above, right*: Blanche Balfour, daughter of Lady Frances and Eustace Balfour, by Sir Edward Burne-Jones: writer and biographer of A J Balfour.

not divide easily into flats - at least into a sufficient number to warrant a developer taking on the project. And the House had a history of problems with the local planning authority which might well have precluded commercial use and, certainly, any permissions would be surrounded by stringent conditions. In the six weeks or so between our first viewing and the closing of offers, Charles Skilton and I hammered out a scheme to bring this once magnificent country house back into residential use.

On the basis of retaining undisturbed and in one unit the enormous public rooms on the ground floor - with their 18 foot- high ceilings - the local planners accepted proposals to create a further five residential apartments within the building. A new lease of life was opened up for a house which had lived, died and was now to be reborn. This is the chequered history of Whittingehame House: a story itself made possible only by the literary energies of its former occupants.

There are a number of extraordinarily vivid accounts of life at Whittingehame and most were written by the women of the family, several of whom were regular correspondents and diarists. Lady Frances Balfour, the former Lady Frances Campbell who married A J Balfour's brother, Eustace, was an extraordinarily perceptive woman as well as a prolific letter writer. She was not only concerned with the life of the family, but was deeply interested in politics and a committed suffragist, as was her sister-in-law, Lady Betty Balfour, married to Gerald Balfour. At the very end of her life Lady Frances published her memoirs, *Ne Obliviscaris*. Her daughter, Blanche, probably inherited some of these qualities from her mother: she not only wrote amusing letters but also two books, her two volume biography of A J Balfour (1936) and *Family Homespun* (1940). In the informed and informative environment of Whittingehame, mothers corresponded with sons and daughters, sisters and sister-in-laws. Very often two or more members of the family give reports, through their correspondence, on the very same events at the House, lending the present day reader a quite unusual insight into the attitudes and characters of members of the family.

Some visitors were more literate than others. Beatrice Webb visited the House and wrote of it in *Our Partnership* (1948). One of the most entertaining of accounts is contained in the diaries of the Eton housemaster and writer, A C Benson. And the local minister, the Reverend Dr Robertson, used the fruits of his many visits to compile his charming and useful little tribute *Lady Blanche Balfour: A Reminiscence* (1897).

There have been a number of biographies of A J Balfour published since the turn of the century, listed in the Bibliography, and I have drawn on these for background material. There is limited material in them relating to home life at Whittingehame as they are predominantly concerned with the public life of the statesman and politician. The information and assumptions as regards Balfour's private life are quite divergent and, in many aspects, inaccurate.

In addition to the published sources and the unpublished diaries and letters, a wealth of material can be gleaned from the study of some of the meticulous records which were kept from time to time and which range from Lady Blanche's Instructions to the Butler (*circa* 1865) to Miss Alice Balfour's Entertainment and Accounts Book (1895-1920). Fortuitously for writers and scholars, the Balfours have in recent times deposited many of these invaluable primary source documents with the Scottish Record Office in Edinburgh and the British Museum in London: the domestic material, for the main-part, being in Edinburgh and the political in London. Thus it is these observers who *really* bring you the story of life in a Scottish country house between the years 1820 and 1935.

"A truly palatial appearance"

In the early part of the 19th century there was a very tangible way to indicate one's arrival in financial and social terms. In the building of a country house the *arriviste* staked his claim in the continuity of the British scene and signified his acceptance of its customs and standards. While not possessing that social cachet of an ancient title, the country house did, nevertheless, at a time of hitherto unequalled social fluidity, secure an *entree* to an exclusive world. New money joined forces with old ideas and attitudes, at the same time as the upholders of traditional values inclined towards commerce. Fuelled by the twin catalysts of social desire and enormous wealth, the practices of the great country house architects of the day flourished as never before . . . .

Against this background, in 1812, James Balfour (1773-1845), second son of John Balfour of Balbirnie, returned to Scotland from India. The Balfour family traced their roots back to Fife in the reign of King Duncan I, in the 11th century, and the grandfather of James was General Robert Balfour of Balbirnie. Young James was consigned to India in 1793 by his father as a clerk in the East India Company: a common fate for the younger sons of landed families. A keen horseman, he was dismissed from the service in 1800, after accepting a present of a fine Arab horse from a local potentate. His undoing was, however, to lead directly to his financial success. He returned to England for a couple of years but then took ship back again - with contracts from the government both to provision the Royal Navy in Indian waters and to supply food for the troops in the event of an outbreak of war. He used this contract very cleverly and, according to Charles Barrington Balfour of Newton Don, "forced the government to apply to him by forseeing the event, and buying up everything in the country."[1] This was his first step to a substantial fortune which, by 1812, amounted to a sum in excess of £300,000. He then left his manager to run the business on a salary of £6,000 a year, which must represent an indication of the considerable health of the enterprise. In London, he was known as 'The Nabob' and he set himself up in style in a house in Grosvenor Square. But, before long, his attention turned to Scotland.

In 1815, he took himself a bride: Eleanor, one of the five daughters of Lord Lauderdale of Thirlestane Castle in Berwickshire. Issue followed quickly and there were to be five children in all. A substantial establishment was clearly required to house Lady Eleanor and their issue and the cheerful financial situation led to him purchasing no less than three properties within two years of their marriage. With little difficulty he acquired the Balgonie estate in his native Fife and the sporting estate of Strathconan in Ross-shire. The acquisition of his third property, which was to be the principal residence, was more problematic. He determined to buy the Ancrum estate from Scott of Ancrum and the purchase was agreed and the deeds drawn up. But, at the very point of signing his name, Scott collapsed and died from a heart attack. His successor obstinately refused to sell and the deal was aborted.

In 1817 he heard that the Whittingehame estate was available and he purchased 10,000 acres of land around Whittingehame from Colonel William Hay of Duns Castle. The Hays of Drumelzier were an old-established local family and had been proprietors of Whittingehame for more than a hundred years. They had come to the area as a result of the marriage in 1695 of the Hon. Lady Elizabeth Seton, heiress of Whittingehame, to the Hon. William Hay of Drumelzier, second son of the first Earl of Tweeddale. There were mixed feelings about the new

5 James Balfour, grandfather of A J Balfour, who ordered the House built in 1817.

6 Sir Robert Smirke, architect of Whittingehame House. Bust by Thomas Campbell, 1845.

laird. "There is pathos in the the record of the sale of Whittingehame after what we believe was an unbroken line of inheritance for more than seven hundred years, through the Earls of Dunbar, the Douglases, the Setons and the Hays, but the pathos is relieved by the fact that the purchaser was a gentleman of such honourable estate, himself to be the progenitor of a distinguished family."[2] Of course, while the direct line of inheritance was indeed broken, through his marriage to Eleanor, the daughter of the 3rd Earl of Lauderdale, the purchase of Whittingehame was not entirely inappropriate for James Balfour.

In short order, Balfour engaged one of the leading architects of the day, Sir Robert Smirke (1780-1867), to build him a mansion house. Smirke enjoyed a substantial reputation as an architect who performed - within budget and on time. He had already been responsible for a number of grand country residences built in classical style, including Kinmount in Dumfriesshire (1812), Newton Don near Kelso (1815), and he had just completed additions to Luton Hoo in Bedfordshire (1816). He had also undertaken with great success, in his Graeco-cubic style, the Covent Garden Theatre (1809, later destroyed). His other great *tour de force* in this field was the British Museum (1823) which was, in turn, followed by the General Post Office building in London (1824), now demolished, equally vast in scale and massively Grecian in style. Smirke was well on his way to a knighthood (1832) and he retired, a wealthy and successful man, in 1845. Somewhat later than Whittingehame he tackled other country house projects, most notably Normanby Park (1825-30), also in a rectilinear Grecian style and visually closely related, and Kinfauns Castle (1820-22), near Perth, in which he reverted to a neo-mediaeval style.

During the period 1801-5, Smirke had travelled extensively in Greece, Italy and Sicily and his sketches there gave him a thorough grounding in the basics of Classical architecture although his first buildings, upon return to England, were mediaeval in style as at Lowther Castle (1806-11) and Eastnor Castle (1810-15). It was the design for Covent Garden Theatre which saw him revert to his classical training with widely recognised success. By 1813, his career had advanced so dramatically as to see him with Soane and Nash as architect to the Board of Works.

His neo-classical style was, in fact, seen at the time as being distinctly modernist although the passage of time perhaps makes us today see it as traditional. Pugin a trifle cynically termed it "the new Square Style of Mr Smirke" and, to a certain extent, it was a reversion to basics rather than being new: the stripping out of superfluous ornamentation and the adoption of simple geometric shapes. As Smirke put it, "Rectangular shapes are the component materials of every modern work." For Mordaunt Crook, from a twentieth century viewpoint, it is rather the case of "an architecture of understatement, poised precariously between promise and platitude. . . his enormous influence channelled the development of the Greek Revival away from the fertile experimentalism of Dance and Sloane, and into the arid wastes of copyism."[3]

Smirke's brief, it would seem, was an architect's dream: the house was quite simply to be larger and more impressive than the family home in Fife, Balbirnie House. Two watercolour artist's impressions of Whittingehame, dated December 4 1817 (now in the collection of the RIBA), show a house of deceptively modest and plain appearance, uncluttered by the later balustrading, and in a sylvan setting. There are also accretions which were not built. Smirke designed Whittingehame in his neo-classical, 'stripped cube' form and incorporated some interesting new techniques into the construction.

Unusually for the time, it was built on a cast-iron framework and, as such, was one of the first, if not *the*

7 Perspective of The Entrance Front, inscr. Albany Decr 4th 1817. An artist's impression in watercolour prepared for the client in Smirke's London office.

8 Perspective of The South Front, inscr. Albany Decr 4th 1817.

first, private house in Britain built in this way. Smirke was one of the pioneers of the use of cast-iron in the framework of buildings and massed concrete in the foundations and successfully combined the now distinct roles of architect and engineer. In Scotland, the first ironworks of importance had been opened at Carron in Stirlingshire in 1760 and it is quite likely that the ironwork used at Whittingehame was cast there, near to Falkirk. The first recorded use of iron in a residential house is for the Doric columns and floorbeams for Nash's extensions to Buckingham Palace (1821), but Whittingehame predates this by three years. Smirke tried out many ideas in the House which he was to modify and incorporate into his later major commission, the British Museum (1823) in London, and which is often referred to in the context of the use of cast-iron. Thus Whittingehame can be seen as something of an experiment in new forms, both structural and architectural.

We know nothing of Smirke's view of his commission. According to Mordaunt Crook, he was a secretive and naturally reticent man. "He was known for his *hauteur*, his dignified indifference, his 'talent for silence'. In true eighteenth-century fashion, he regarded architectural composition as a private matter between architect and patron..."⁴

We do know that the local red sandstone in East Lothian was not deemed to be of a high enough standard for Whittingehame and the grey, fine-grained Cullalo freestone was quarried at Cullels Quarry near Burntisland in Fife, brought over to Dunbar harbour by barge

9 Aerial view of Whittingehame House, entrance front from the north.

and thence transported uphill to the site on carts drawn by oxen and horses. There, James Dorward, builder of Haddington, erected the magnificent edifice according to the instructions of Smirke and and his site representatives. Dorward remarked, with evident awe, to the contractors for the cartage - Alexander of Yarrow and Alexander of Newmains - that it was the only house he ever built where the cartage of the stones was paid by weight.

Upon its completion, it was reckoned to be one of the grandest houses in Scotland, massive in effect, and is to this day regarded as one of the finest of extant neo-classical country houses, carefully set in its own parkland. "There are three noble approaches, each of great length, winding through beautiful scenery and guarded by handsome lodges"[5]. A local historian, Croal, was obviously deeply impressed, " the mansion on all sides wears a truly palatial appearance."[6] That having been said, a later visitor, Margot Tennant, was less complimentary, "The classical style of Whittingehame appeared to me better suited to municipal buildings."[7] In no way could it ever have been thought of as a pretty house: it is without much in the way of ornamentation, inside or outside, and has none of the practised opulence which so often characterises the British country house. But that notwithstanding, it represented the height of fashion when it was built although one of A J Balfour's biographers took an overtly caustic view: ". . . a large undistinguished block of masonry rather resembling a section of one of the older squares of Brighton . . . and what tradition clings about the spot has no relation to the Balfours." But then, one of A J Balfour's contemporary biographers, E T Raymond, abhorred what he disparagingly termed "new money".[8]

Smirke's basic design and layout was the essence of simplicity, as indeed demanded by the style he had adopted. There was a high rectilinear central block with a slightly lower extension on either side. The central block on the north-east facade comprised four storeys, including the basement, fronted by an elegant *porte cochere*, with a canopy supported by a row of four fluted Doric columns all in a row, after the style of the Temple of Theseus at Athens (465 BC), protruding from the middle part of the ground floor. The windows were plain and regular in position, large enough to allow a generous amount of light into the rooms within and most were surmounted by simple cornices. The whole was completed by plain string courses between the storys and parapets of classical curved balusters, which do not appear in the architect's impressions.

"What makes it interesting is that Smirke built it all

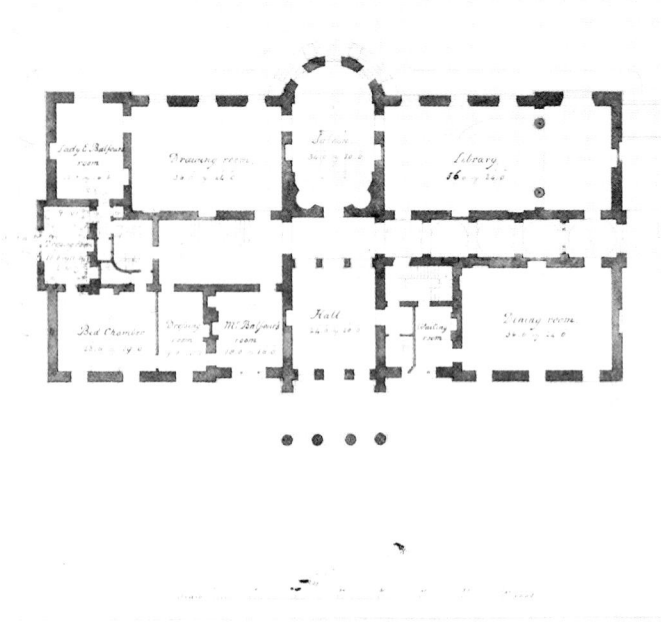

up from slabs of one-bay thickness in such a way as to give depth to the centre part and length to the side parts, and to the whole thing an intriguing variety of scale and silhouette."[9]

The south-east facade continued the classical features of the north front, variety being attained by projecting the middle part of the ground floor beyond the main wall line and featuring a tripartite window, the part above recessed so as to make the end of the building appear as two wings, giving the surmounting balustrades full play.

The south facade featured a handsome central curved bay window with a classical balustraded parapet above, in the same position as the porch at the front. Leading down from this feature a set of steps was later constructed, onto a terrace (now enclosed by balustrading all erected 1871-72). The ground on the south side was also excavated later to a depth of six feet, allowing light to enter the basement rooms previously shrouded in the darkness of a moat. The excavated earth was used to widen the terrace and three sets of steps were built; one set in the middle down to the lower terrace and two at either side. A conservatory, with facility to enter from the lib-

10 Plan of the Principal Story, by Smirke, 1817.

rary in the main house, was originally built on what is now an upper terrace (only the arcaded rear wall remains). A pedimented Greek Doric *loggia* was built at the south-west corner - to be imitated in 1827 by Burn with a similar construction on the north front.

The north east-facing facade of the House, although incorporating the main entrance, does not enjoy a great deal in the way of sun, except in the early mornings, and so the sunny, terraced south west facade has tended over the years to be regarded as the 'front' of the House. The large astragalled windows in this latter elevation would originally have lent an uninterrupted view of rolling parkland but in the last 150 years fine, mature trees - copper beech, cypress and oak - have obscured this view without impeding the sun which pours in through the windows in spring and summer.

The arrangement of the rooms was straightforward and symmetrical with reception rooms on the ground floor, together with separate bedrooms and dressing rooms for Lady Eleanor Balfour and James Balfour. The rest of the bedroom accommodation was on the first floor, or 'Chamber Story'. The House was built around two *axes*: the shorter being that which continues beyond

11 Plan of the Chamber Story, by Smirke, 1817.

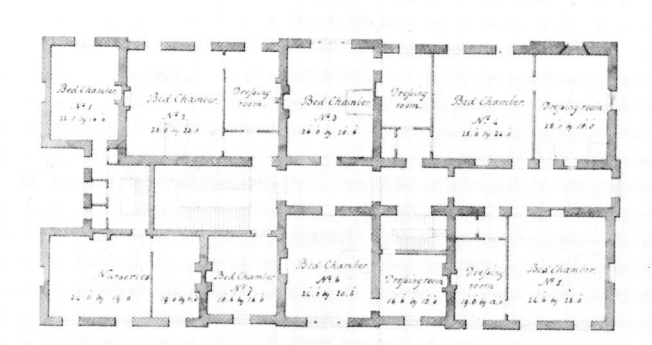

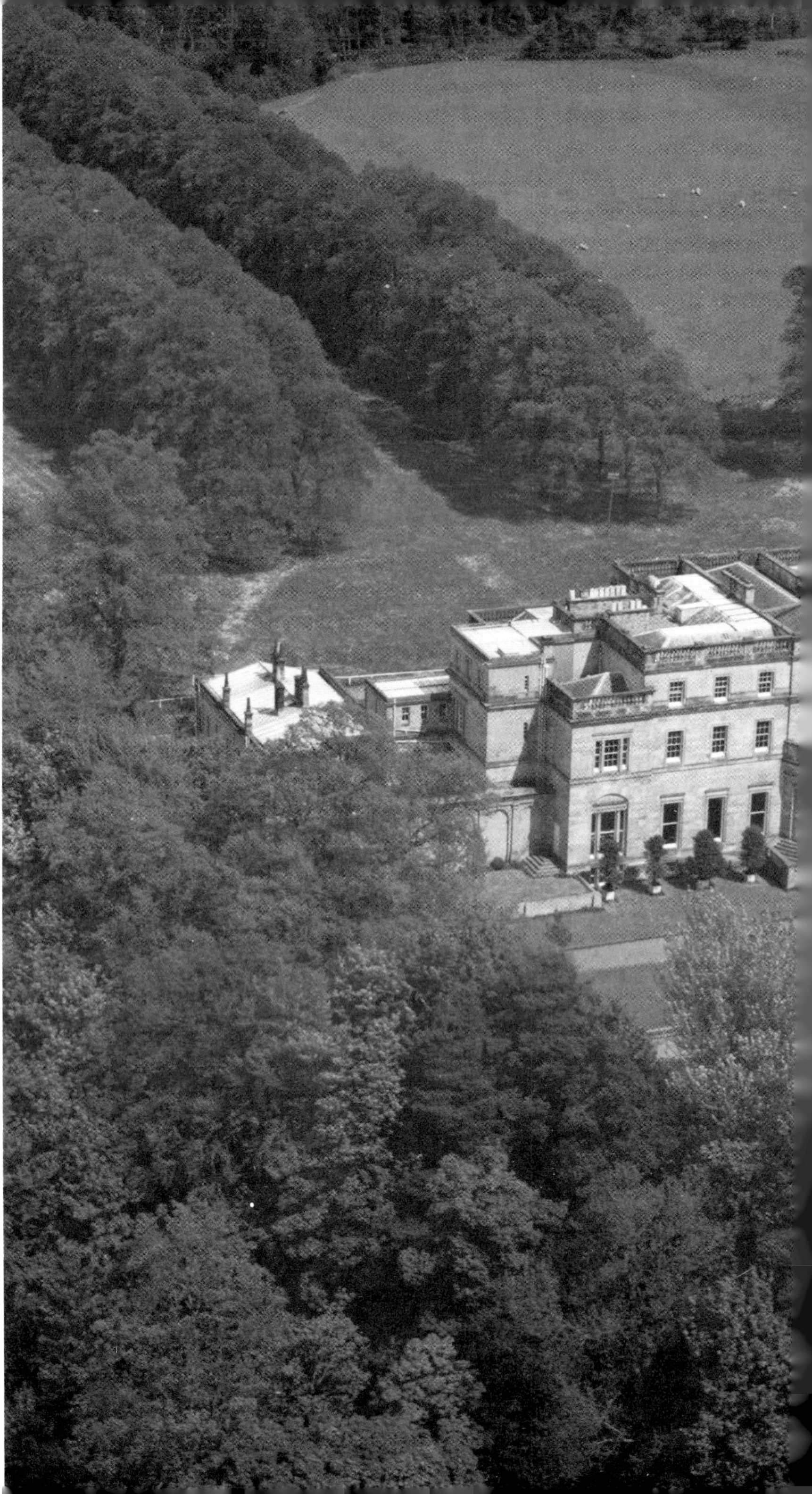

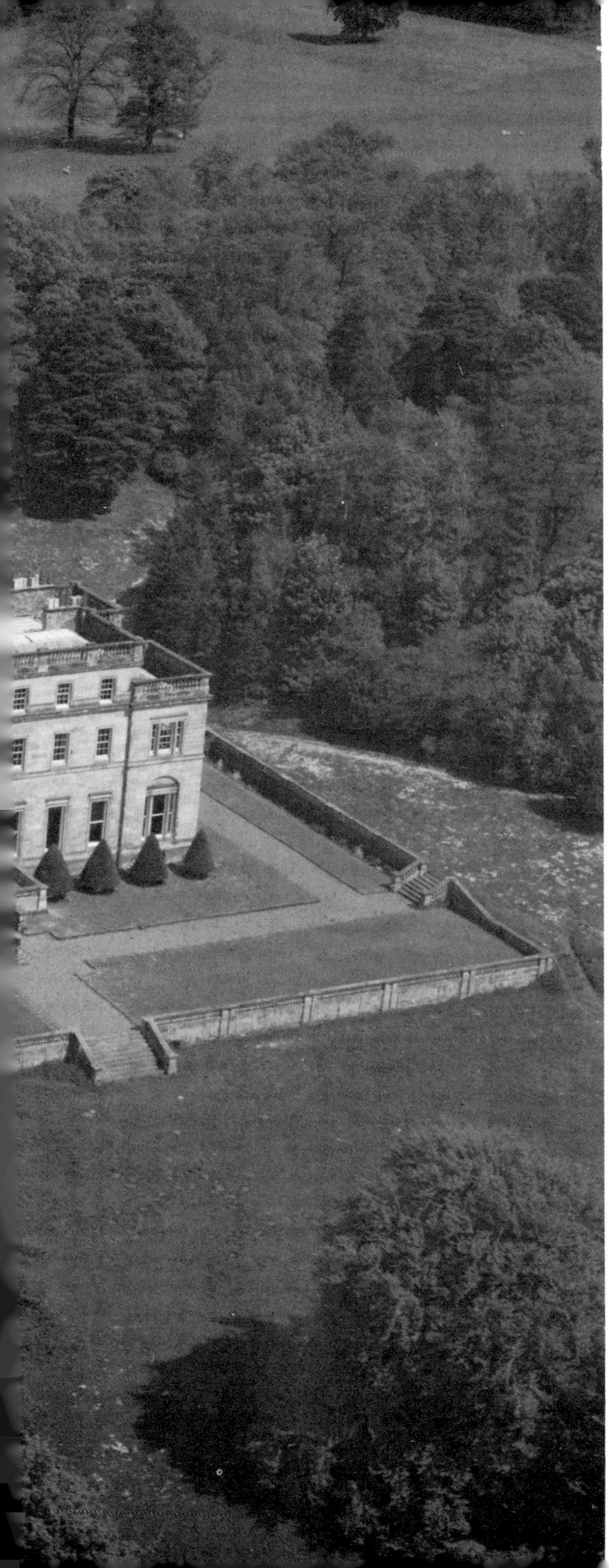

the entrance hall, with its black Doric chimney piece and its *anta* screen beyond, into the Saloon (later known as the Music Room) and out to the back.

The longer axis is the main ground floor corridor with its five high saucer domes. This feature brings to mind many features of the British Museum, particularly Smirke's Arch Room (1841). Running off the corridor on the garden side is the very large main Library of the House with its two Doric columns and ceiling in five coffered sections. The shelves of the library were filled as part of the original furnishing contract with good leather: "works of unquestionable literary orthodoxy."[10]

On the other side of the corridor is the dining room which was remodelled in 1899 with carved ceiling and walls panelled in Japanese oak. Prior to the remodelling, it had plain, painted walls upon which hung family portraits and, above the black marble fireplace, a large heavy oil of Joseph and his children.

Beyond the library and up three steps is the single storey extension added later by Burn and which was used a second library. It is a large north-facing room, cold in feeling, mitigated only by the ornate Grecian style ceiling with its sunken, diagonal-ribbed centre surrounded by laurel moulding.

At the opposite end of this main corridor is the stair which leads to what were the principal bedrooms on the first floor. To the right of the stair, on the ground floor, is the large and sunny south facing drawing room with its coffered ceiling in six sections. The drawing room was deliberately placed, according to the custom of the time, on the other side of the saloon and down the corridor from the dining room so as to provide state and distance for the formal procession into dinner, and in order that the sound of the gentlemen at their port and cigars after the meal might not disturb the ladies in the drawing room. The room off the drawing room was used variously as Lady Eleanor Balfour's room, a billiard room and as Miss Alice Balfour's business room.

To the left, on the north-east corner, is the study, later to be known as 'Mr Balfour's Room', and which was originally James Balfour's room. The ceiling of this room was most probably reworked at the same time as the remodelling of the dining room, in 1899. Here, A J Balfour kept his working books. Modern history was well represented and a collection of books on metaphysics and philosophy reflected early, and continuing, interests. Books on the Irish question reflected his second government appointment. In the smaller proportions of the study, Balfour found more comfort than in the vast proportions of

12 *Previous page*: Aerial view of Whittingehame House, south facade.

the library. Here, in the study, he wrote his most significant book, *The Foundations of Belief*, at a large mahogany writing desk of American design. An iron grand pianoforte stood in another corner. As A J Balfour was accustomed to working late into the night, and sleeping consequently late into the morning, he often did not retire to the principal bedroom on the first floor, but occupied a small room off the study when he became tired. On the other side of his study was a small dressing room, and beyond it the room created in 1901 and known as the book room and which came into use as an informal meeting room for the family.

The three arches high on the landing of the main stair originally contained oriental porcelain on their heavily scrolled Baroque style brackets. The arches, the centre rosette in the cupola and the egg and dart moulding are the only concessions to ornamentation in the otherwise severe and plain design of Smirke. The stairwell itself is a vast and impressive space well lit by the enormous cupola which is set into a flat lead section of the roof. When James Balfour and his family moved in the stair area was hung with large tapestries suspended from the brass rails which can still be seen high above. Cleaning of the rails and ledges in this area must have been a hazardous undertaking ! At the second floor level on the west side is a gallery with ironwork matching that on the stairs and which connected to the three servants' bedrooms on the south side of the house and one rather more superior bed chamber on the north side. During the time of great house parties, children of the House would peer from behind the balcony at the adults in their finery descending the main staircase to dinner. In the most recent conversion work this balcony has been retained as a feature but the three entrances to it sealed up.

The first floor of the House, the 'Chamber Story' on Smirke's plans, was given over to bedrooms and dressing rooms for family and guests and the nurseries which were the domain of the children, their tutor, governesses and the nursery servants. In such large establishments, the children were kept out of the sight and the hearing of the adults. The bedrooms were of generous proportion but their simplicity was to be altered after A J Balfour took over: the plain Italian marble fireplaces would remain only in the nursery wing and would be replaced elsewhere by heavy late Victorian fireplaces and overmantel superstructures. All the bedrooms for family and guest use had dressing rooms opening off them. The servants' rooms were not so appointed. Accessed by a back stair on the north side of the bedroom corridor was the servants' accommodation on the top floor or attic storey; six less comfortable rooms given over to dormitory type accommodation, with more comfortable Bed Chambers for the more senior staff like the butler, housekeeper and steward.

The vast basement of the house was a world all of its own, made up of an enormous, high servants' hall, kitchen, store rooms, still room, coal cellars, steward's room, butler's room, butler's cleaning room (with plate room off), housekeeper's room (with china room off), wine cellars (76 bins in all) and a large beer cellar. In the basement corridor there was the bell board which was connected to every room in the House by a wire and crank system of bells.

Across the courtyard, within Smirke's classical *loggia*, was a bakehouse and a brewhouse and within the service court there were stores for bottles, coal and ashes, of which last there would have been a great quantity every morning after the cleaning of the grates.

The interior of the house was finished to a standard fully in keeping with the opulence of the exterior. At the beginning of 1819, the family moved in, "almost before the mortar was dry" [7]. The rooms were filled with elegant

13 Plan of the Attic Story, by Smirke, 1817.

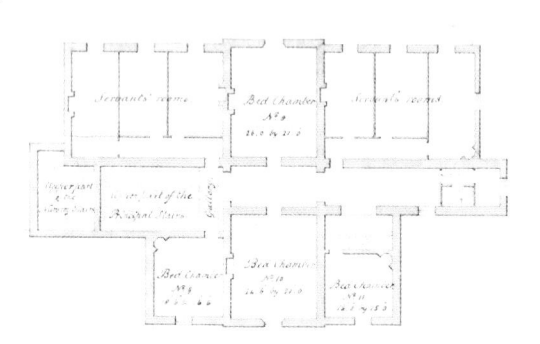

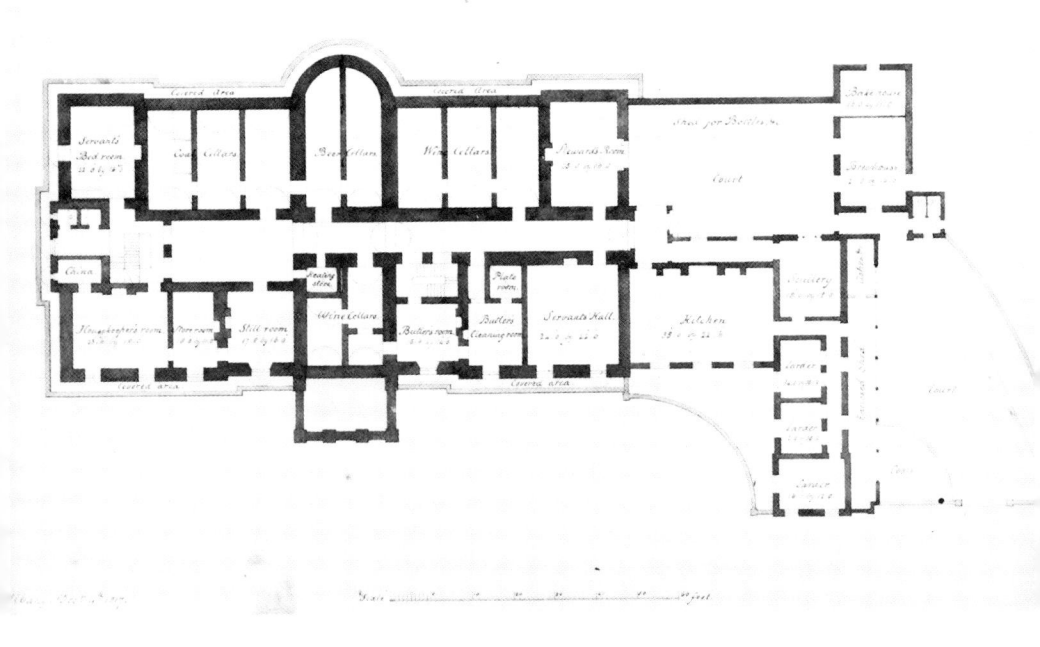

14 Plan of the Basement Story, by Smirke, 1817.

and ornate French furniture, after the style of the time. There were buhl cabinets, Sevres china and French clocks decorated with ormolu figures representing scenes from mythology. The saloon and drawing room walls were covered with primrose yellow, patterned brocade. All this opulence was provided with James Balfour's "new gold".[8]

James Balfour, late of Balbirnie and India, readily adopted the lifestyle of the country gentleman in the company of his blue-blooded consort, daughter of the Earl of Lauderdale. The entertaining was lavish. In the 1920s, Lady Elizabeth Countess of Airlie recalled an account of a visit by her mother-in-law to Whittingehame House in 1843, during their occupancy. Lady Eleanor was "in full panoply of bare shoulders, diamonds, crinoline and lace flounces." There were many grand guests and stately drives around the surrounding countryside in the Whittingehame *barouche*.[11]

The gardens and parkland were laid out around 1819 to the instructions of the noted gardener and arborist William S Gilpin (1762-1843), nephew of William Gilpin and whose family was associated with the Smirkes. The two families were, in fact, related and Smirke's father had been taught drawing by Captain J B Gilpin. The younger Gilpin had a substantial English and Irish practice and the Smirke introduction brought him a rather smaller Scottish one, which developed after his work at Whittingehame and Kinfauns. It would appear that this early work was much acclaimed for he went on to commissions at Bowhill, Drumlanrig Castle, Dalkeith Palace and Dunmore, amongst many others. Whittingehame is a noted example of Gilpin's work in that he was remarkably successful at creating a landscape setting for the Grecian mansion house.

Gilpin divided scenic design into five distinct categories: the Grand, the Romantic, the Beautiful, the Picturesque and the Rural. Whittingehame was created in his Picturesque style, described in his *Hints on Landscape Gardening*, as "marked by smaller and more abrupt folds of grounds, with but little flat surface, and clothed in a rougher mantle." There were three magnificent drives, to east, south and west. Two of these were very long approaches at the side of the Whittingehame Water. The main approach ran from the lodge at Ruchlaw Mill alongside the water, crossed it by a simple, rustic wooden bridge and later went over the public road, carried by a substantial stone arch, to come out in flat parkland to the north front of the house. The other waterside approach ran from the lodge on the Garvald road, up and through a delightful ravine before emerging into rolling parkland, with the ancient Tower to the left and the splendid south front of the House ahead. The Tower was employed as a decorative feature, visible from both approach and from the windows of the reception rooms of the House. Across the Water, a walled fruit and vegetable garden was established; also greenhouses, a curvilinear-roofed peachery and vineries. There were herbaceous borders and fruit gardens. The stables, on the service drive as one approaches the house, were built to Smirke's design and, of the four surviving lodges, the L-shaped neo- classical east lodge, its walls broken by *antae* and with a pediment on each gable, and the west lodge would both appear to also have been his work. The later, curious Half Moon Lodge, at the foot of the present drive, was demolished in the late 1960's and its sought-after facing stone incorporated in some other building at nearby Gullane. Near to the foot of the service drive was an ice house, a stone vaulted chamber into which the winter ice was packed, insulated between layers of straw, for use throughout the summer.

The old Tower was within the grounds of the House. It was, and is, a fortified tower house of ancient construc-

15 *Right*: The West lodge, by Smirke (1818).

16 *Far right*: The East lodge, by Smirke (1818).

17 Aerial view of the Stable block, by Smirke (1818). The stables were extended twice: the first extension being to the two legs *(foreground)* and the second (1859) by building out the north east front.

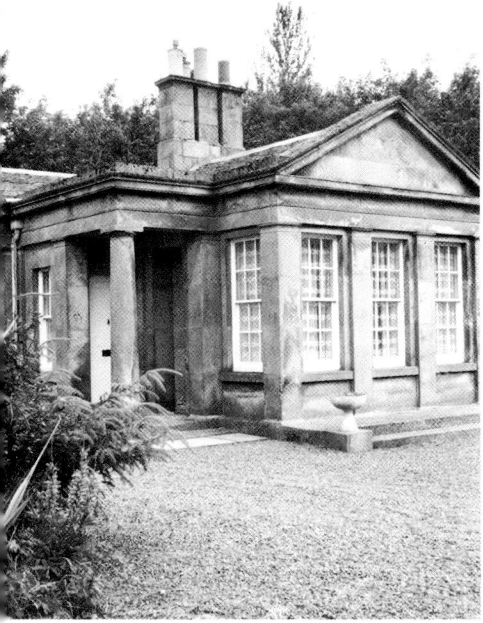

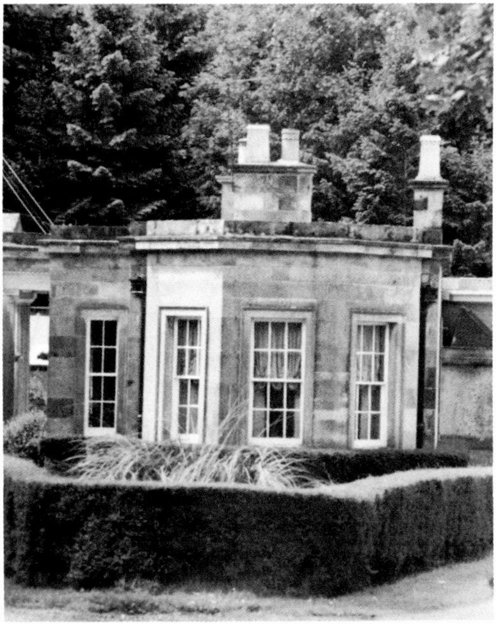

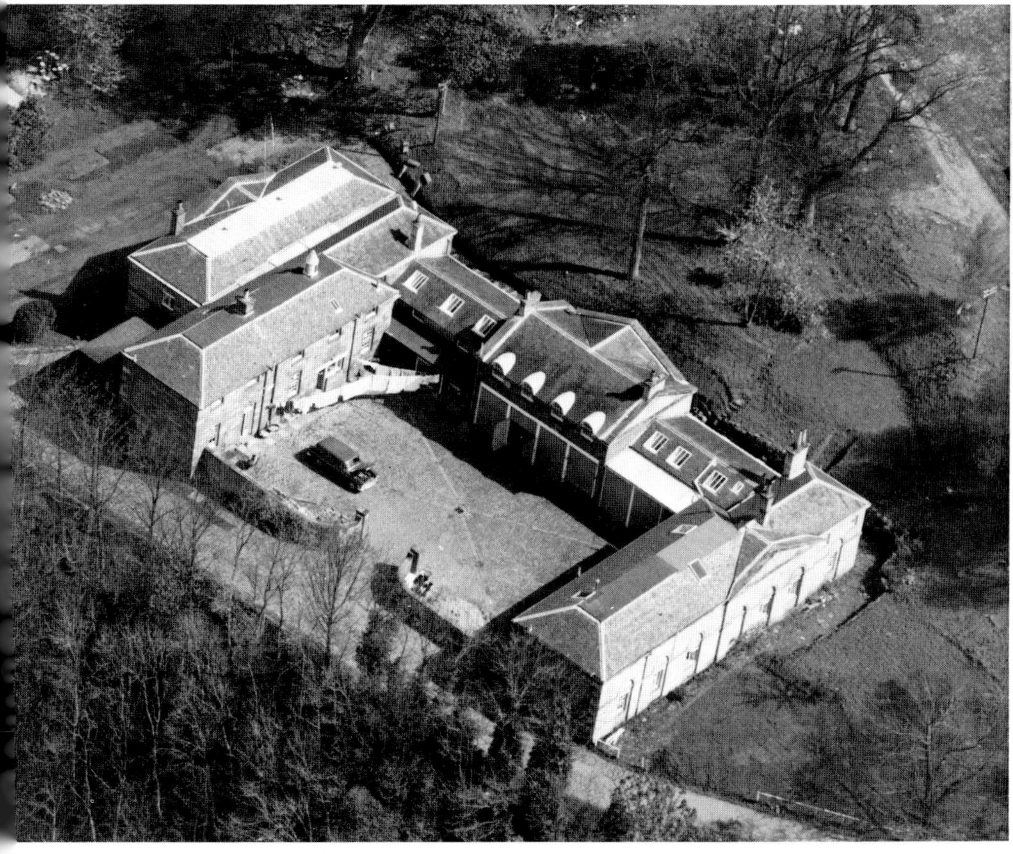

Whittinghame Tower from S.E.

tion, some parts possibly as old as the late 15th century but its origins are not documented and writers tend to disagree over the extent of its antiquity. It is basically rectangular in plan with a staircase wing on the north side. A western single storey extension to the Tower was brought into use by the Balfours as a laundry for the House. Ornate plaster ceilings had been modelled in some of the Tower rooms: it is believed by the same artists as executed the decorated ceilings at Winton House, near Pencaitland, around 1625. After 1900, Miss Alice Balfour took in hand the further restoration of the Tower: an ornate hidden ceiling was uncovered and the ivy was stripped from the walls. For many years it was used as a bothy for unmarried estate workers and a small museum was created. There are also a number of later additions, as a result of it being brought back into residential use by the Balfour family in 1964, when they moved from Redcliff.

The Tower was originally built by the Douglas family and here in 1567, according to popular legend, the murder of Darnley was plotted by Bothwell, Lethington and the fourth Earl, later the Regent Morton, below the spreading branches of the great yew tree which still survives. Near to the Tower, within what were originally the grounds of the House, is a walled garden with ornamental wrought iron gates (1915), a temple (1905) and the family graveyard. The two 18th-century entrance pillars

18 Whittingehame Tower from the south east, postcard view *circa* 1905.

19 The later Half Moon Lodge (demolished 1964).

and lodges, all of local red sandstone, predate the takeover of the Whittingehame estate by James Balfour and the well worn stone bears the coat of arms of the Hays. The eastmost lodge building was extended after the estate changed hands - most probably *circa* 1830 - and a neoclassical frontage was added on the south side at which time it became the gardener's cottage.

The grounds between the House and the Tower are dissected naturally by a deep ravine through which flows the Whittingehame Water which rises in the parish of Garvald where it is known as the Garvald Water or the Nunraw Burn. It is also known as the River Papana, as the Beil Burn at Biel, and where it flows to the sea at Belhaven it is the Belhaven or Belton Water. The fine old trees which graced its banks all contributed to the general scenic effect developed by Gilpin. The whole effect was much enhanced by the creation of a large artificial lake to the southeast of the House, Pressmennan Lake (1819).

The old village of Whittingehame, with its mill by the edge of the Whittingehame Water near the present stone bridge, its school, its public house, its brewery, three shops, five smiths, four masons, six wrights, eight shoemakers, four tailors and four weavers, was effectively annexed and removed by James Balfour. The site of the village was incorporated into the Whittingehame estate, in works which must have been controversial at the time. The parish church was retained on the same site on which it had stood since 1722 but was largely rebuilt in 1820 on the instructions of James Balfour in a battlemented Gothic style on a T-plan. Whittingehame had, in its day, been a place of note, although it was suffering from a degree of dilapidation which might well have justified its effective destruction. Traditionally, Cromwell's soldiery, on the march from Danskine to Dunbar, drank the brewery dry ! Around 1830, James Balfour had several more modern houses erected on a site one mile to the north in the valley of the Luggate Burn - the location of the present village - and, in 1831, work was begun there on a new schoolhouse. Above the site of the old village, further construction was started on the house of Redcliff, built in Jacobean style of local red sandstone, and Lady Eleanor's cottage, created as a sewing school for the ladies of the immediate area. The manse by the church was built much later in the 1870's.

The Scottish architect William Burn (1789-1870) had been apprenticed to Smirke's London practice in 1808 and in that office he was fully trained in the neo-classical style, his work including the supervision of the building of the peviously mentioned Covent Garden Theatre. He returned to Scotland in 1811 where he took on the building of Smirke's first Scottish country house, Kinmount. Thereafter, he set up in practice on his own account in George Street in Edinburgh, attracting a wide range of commissions ranging fron the North Leith Church, the Customs House at Greenock and the Edinburgh Academy building to the Dundas Monument in Edinburgh's St Andrews Square. But it was his country house practice which was to flourish above all and it is hardly surprising that he received an approach in 1826 from James Balfour, newly installed at Whittingehame. It is difficult to ascertain the extent of involvement, if any, Burn had already had with the House, although it is not unreasonable to suspect that he had taken considerable interest in the progress of Smirke's mansion house. In the absence of Smirke in London it is quite likely, in view of Burn's proximity to the construction site, that the latter assisted to some degree in the control and progress of the project.

It might be reasonable to suspect that the family found Smirke's house somewhat austere and uncompromising and, in 1826, Burn was engaged to add ornate ceilings in library, saloon and drawing room. The single storey extension, wing and Greek *loggia* which stand to the west of the main building were also added as further accommodation, particularly domestic offices, were required. This he achieved, it can be seen from his plans dated January 2 1827, by building on top of the existing kitchen and basement offices, adding a further two floors' accommodation, and fronting with a portico like that of Smirke, which already existed on the south side of the building. The block projected in front of the general line of the main building and was terminated by an arcade, the roof of which was supported in front by four Doric columns, round and plain, carrying a plain architrave and

20 William Burn's extension for domestic offices, 1827.

21 Elevation of the west wing by William Burn (1827).

22 *Overleaf*: William Burn's elevation of the entrance front incorporating his changes (1827).

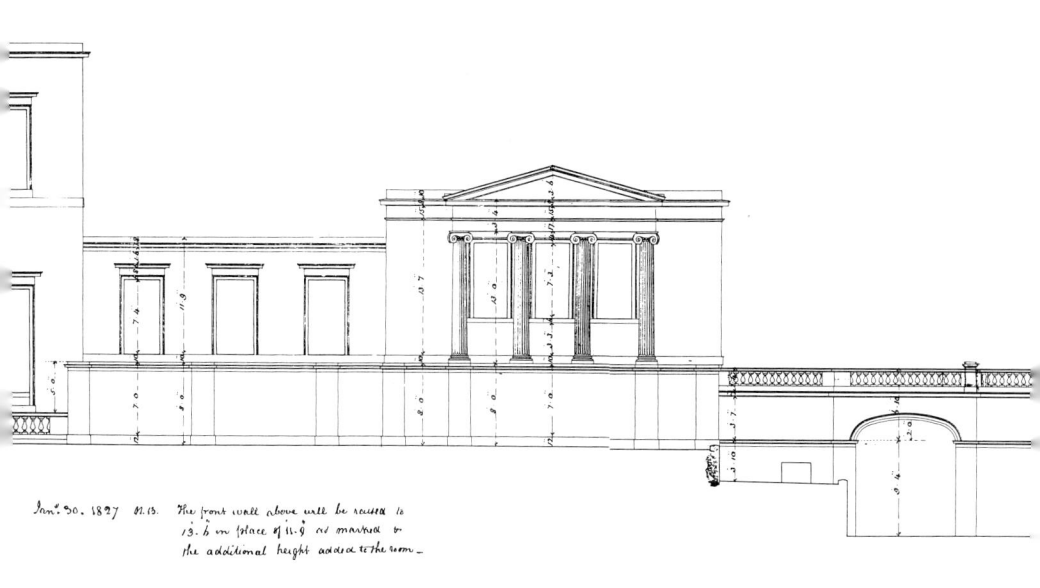

Jan. 30. 1827 No. 13. The front wall above will be raised to
13.6 in place of 11.9 as marked &
the additional height added to the room —

Whittinghame N.º 8
Elevation of the Entrance Front

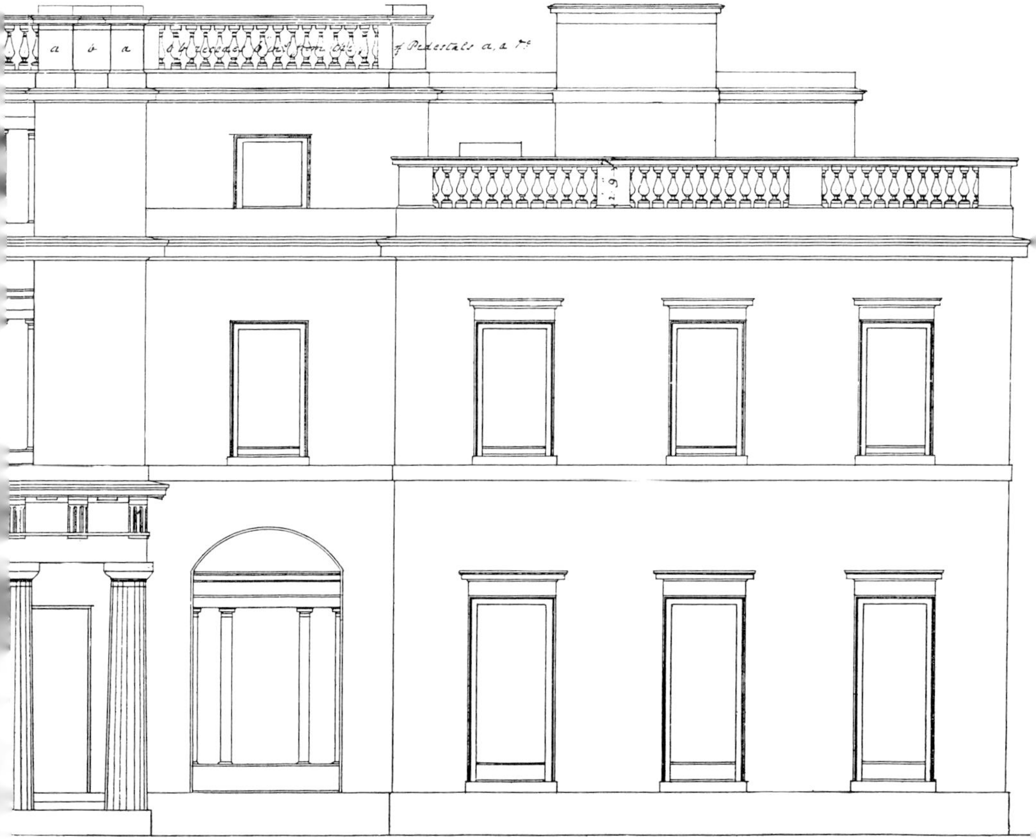

a
b
a
recessed
of Pedestals a, a

a pediment. An arched and balustraded entrance to the service courtyard at the side was also added. He also built two great piers, flanking the centre bay of the main block, and a deep plinth and encircled the whole building with balustrading.

A very large and grand House had been created but the classical simplicity of Smirke's original concept was already quite ruined.

"An event of no small importance..."

The son and heir to the Whittingehame estate, James Maitland Balfour, was born on January 5 1820. He was, in fact, the second son, the first having died tragically in a fire in infancy very shortly after the House was first occupied. The infant, John, was burned in his bed at Whittingehame: it is said a spark from his mother's candle, as she leaned over him, caused the bedclothes to catch light. The birth of James was followed by Charles (1824-72), who inherited Balgonie in Fife, and who was later to purchase Newton Don near Kelso which, coincidentally, was also designed by Smirke. (This latter property had belonged to the Dons for more than 250 years but Sir William Don sold the property, married an actress and went on the stage.) There were also two daughters: Mary and Anne.[12]

After education at Eton and Trinity College, Cambridge, James Balfour married, at the age of 23, Lady Blanche Gascoigne Cecil. The bride was 18 years old but already remarkably self-possessed. He was marrying into one of the great families of England: the Cecils having occupied a position in the centre of the political and social stage since Elizabethan times. Lady Blanche was a daughter of the second Marquis of Salisbury and sister to the future Prime Minister, the third Marquis. Upon his father's death in 1847, four years after their marriage, James Maitland Balfour succeeded to the house and estate of Whittingehame and he and his wife made their home there. Lady Blanche was widely regarded as an asset to the community: the Rev. James Robertson observed, perhaps a trifle sycophantically, "Her doings and movements gave that stir to country life and that brightness which comes of its routine being pleasantly broken, and the people had the interest in her which they always have in youth, courage and frankness".[13]

The new laird also played an active part in the local community, sitting in the House of Commons as a member for the Haddington Burghs. He was also Chairman of the North British Railway Company and Major-Commandant of the East Lothian Yeomanry Cavalry. His years

23 *Overleaf*: Whittingehame House, north entrance front, photograph *circa* 1870. Note the *porte cochere* which allows carriages to draw up under cover. This was infilled, 1901.

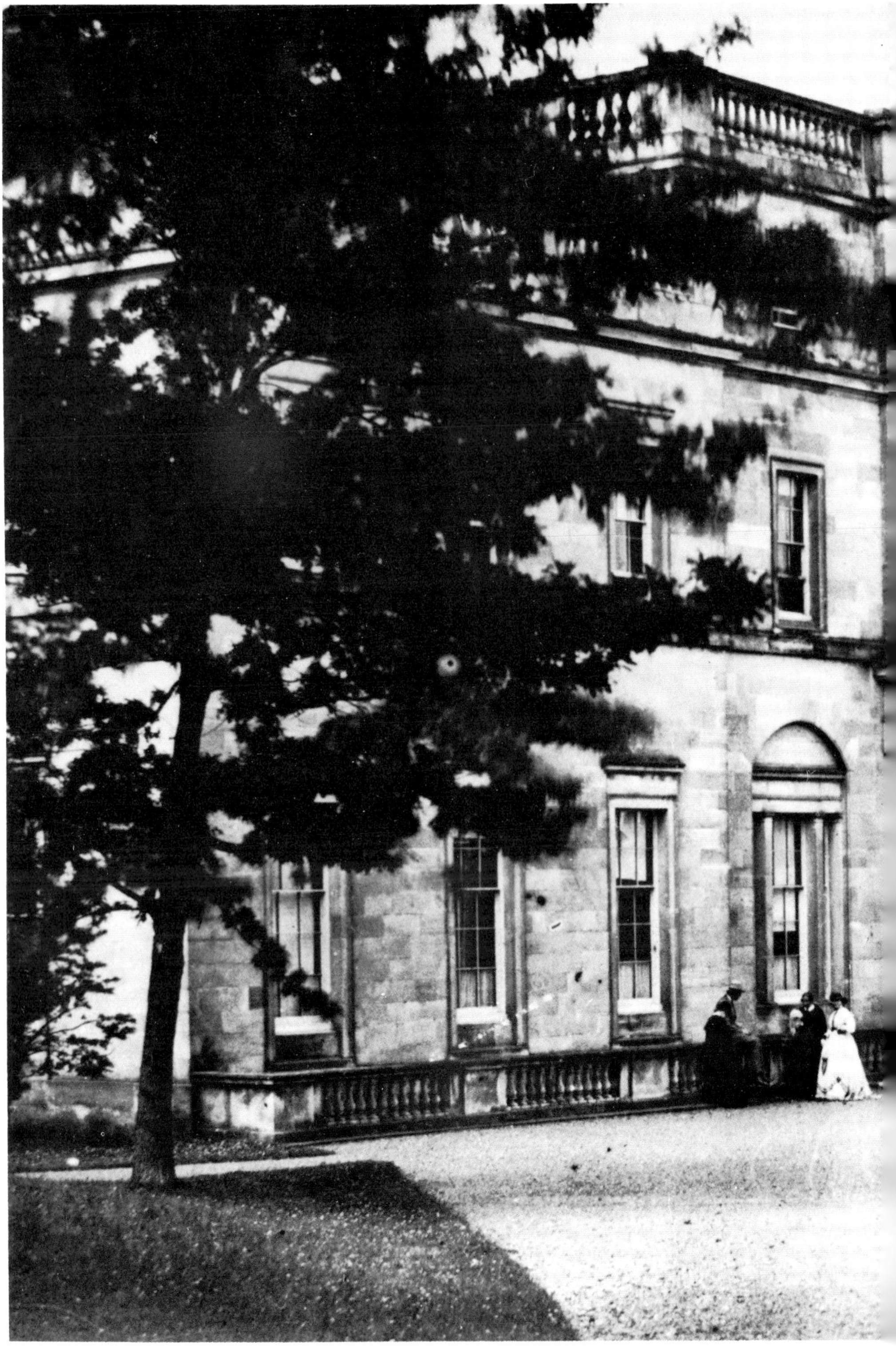

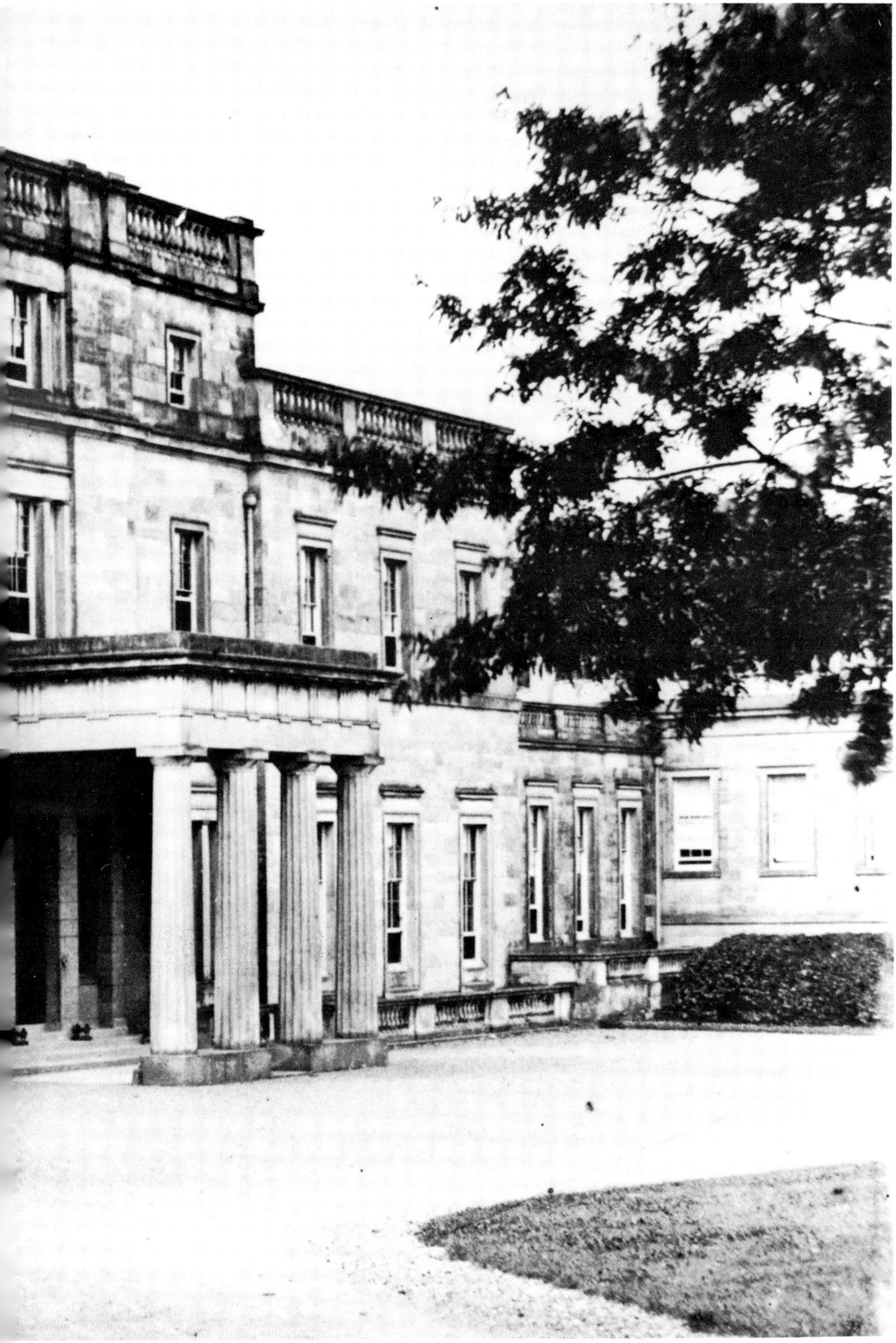

were, however, to be cut short. He became ill in 1854 - according to one story breaking a blood vessel in a paroxysm of coughing whilst dressing in his uniform of the East Lothian Yeomanry. Tuberculosis developed and he effectively became an invalid. Passing the kitchen one day, his daughter Evelyn espied a live turtle crawling on the flagstones and, asking the cook what the creature was, was told it was to be turned into a soup to make her father better. The turtle did not effect a miraculous cure and after a protracted and chronic illness he died in Madeira, where he was buried, in 1856. At Blaikeyheugh, some two miles away, in a suitably commanding position overlooking Traprain Law and the countryside all around, a handsome sandstone obelisk was raised in the year 1858 by the Yeomanry in memory of their dead commander and inscribed with evident affection and respect:

> To the memory of James Maitland Balfour, Esquire of Whittingehame, Major Commandant of the East Lothian Yeomanry Cavalry, by the Officers, Non-Commissioned Officers, and Privates of the Corps, in testimony of their great respect and esteem for him as a Commanding Officer, of their affectionate regard for him as an amiable and able country gentleman, and of their deep and lasting regret for his premature removal from among them.

24 James Maitland Balfour, father of A J Balfour, painted at the age of 17 by George Richmond.

25 Lady Blanche Balfour, mother of A J Balfour, painted at the age of 22 by James R Swinton.

In thirteen years of marriage, Lady Blanche had borne nine children and upon return from Madeira, she set about, with her characteristic great vigour, the upbringing of her surviving eight children: five sons and three daughters. The oldest son, Arthur James Balfour, had been born on July 25 1848 and was destined for great office and the widest recognition, as philosopher, politician and Prime Minister. The fortitude of his mother must have been a considerable influence in the shaping of statesman and thinker and life at Whittingehame, in the absence of the male head of the household, must have placed particular strains upon both Lady Blanche and the oldest son.

Some of the great public rooms of the House were now locked up except on special occasions and the fine French furniture disappeared under dust-covers. The nurseries and schoolrooms on the first floor now became the focus of life and activity for Lady Blanche and her eight children. The novels of Jane Austen were brought up from the library below: these were the favourites of both mother and offspring. A tutor and two governesses from Switzerland - Amalie and Auguste Kling - were engaged for the education of the children and Lady Blanche was assisted by a family retainer from Hatfield, the aptly named Miss Emily Faithfull. Although the establishment was considerably reduced and there was now little entertaining, high standards were observed domestically under the keen eye of Lady Blanche who, no doubt, subscribed to the religiously based view of the time, "Exhort servants to be obedient unto their own masters, and to please them in all things" (*Titus* ii.9).

In 1856, she started a small book of Instructions to the Butler which, inscribed in her own hand, lays down detailed instructions for the running of the house. There is little latitude for misinterpretation: "The butler will give in a weekly report every Saturday at 1/2 p. 12. In any absence he will forward it by post." The procedure for dealing with the books and bills is laid down as is the payment of the servants: livery servants and butler, quarterly, others weekly. The clocks were to be regularly wound, "Edinburgh Railway Time to be kept." Newspapers "as soon as they have been opened and smoothed out will be placed in the Library . . . *The Spectator* and other weekly newspapers will remain a week on the library table." At the end of the week, local newspapers were then to be taken to the factors and *Chambers Journal* to the gardeners. The Butler's tasks seem never ending: to weigh and stamp outgoing mail; take up incoming mail; the charge of the lighting, both gas and the lamps; to check stationery supplies in library, study, sitting rooms and bedrooms; get in coals for house and laundry; and charge of the front door and the back door of the conservatory in the library and the responsibility for the closing of the shutters in all the public rooms at night.

The purchase and control of all drink within the House was another important responsibility. Sherry was to be bought in small quantities, stocks of port and wine to be maintained and their withdrawal from the cellar noted in a book specially kept for the purpose. Bottled and 'draft' ales and beers were kept and drunk in pints. "The spirit drunk in the house is whiskey (sic). Whiskey toddy is drunk in the steward's room at supper time." The instructions are detailed as to how much alcohol is allowed to each of the servants with male servants allowed to drink roughly twice as much as female servants. But Lady

26 Lady Blanche and her family at the front of the house, *circa* 1866.

Blanche warns, "Take care that strict sobriety is maintained and that no spirits are drunk in the Hall."

The upstairs footman and his lad are to be dressed in livery and there are instructions for the purchase and the keeping of uniforms. The butler has charge of the plate, the glasses and the cutlery but he is let off the hook when it comes to the china. "The china in this house is mostly of great value and the housekeeper is responsible for it."[14]

At one stage all the children - one by one - contracted diptheria and their friend the eminent doctor, Sir James Simpson, had to be summoned repeatedly from Edinburgh by the despatch of the coachman from Whittingehame. All the children survived with much nursing but those at one of the farms on the estate were less lucky - eight died. Lady Blanche developed a ploy which, by all accounts, greatly assisted recovery. A family newspaper was started, the *Whittinghame Advertiser*, and all the children were called upon to contribute to the manuscript paper. It survived during the Christmas and New Year holiday periods for two years and was read aloud, "in full conclave", every week. There is still a drawer in a cupboard outside A J Balfour's former study and which bears, in his own hand, the legend, *Whittinghame Advertiser*.

The three series of the newspaper, fortunately preserved to this day, give a most remarkable insight into the life and running of a mid-Victorian country house. The first appearance of the newspaper is portentously announced in a poster-sized sheet of manuscript produced in January 1864 as "an event of no small importance in the annals of our county." The first issue is dated February 1 1864 and the manuscript newspaper contains all the news of the House - "Almost all the rooms are at present occupied by invalids" - plus articles on the surrounding area. Issue number two is already a more sophisticated journalistic effort with more news, poetry, *A Romance* by A J B and E M B (Arthur and brother Eustace) and letters, including a witty and quite hilarious pastiche of a complaining letter from the editor of the *Haddingtonshire Courier*, expostulating against the new publication and its inherent threat to professionals. In succeeding issues we learn of the gradual recovery of the children.

The second series of newspapers is published over the Christmas and New Year of 1866-7 and reports that "the corridor, hall, dining-room and library were as usual magnificently decorated with holly and other evergreens, on Christmas eve . . . the abundance of holly berries this year have rendered the decorations particularly successful." On Christmas Day two "pleasant and noisy games of poole (sic.)" are noted and it was recorded with evident approval that "a handsome gas stove has been put up at the end of the corridor" and that it was far more successful than the rocking horse last year - presumably at keeping the inhabitants warm ! The only occurrence of great drama appears to have been a fire caused by a piece of phosphorous in one of the children's bedrooms, as a result of which "several people were employed until a late hour of the night endeavouring to extinguish it." There is an important, official announcement:

> We are authorised to state that the treat to be given to the Sunday school-children will take place on Wednesday or Saturday in next week. The proceedings will be as follows - At four o'clock, the children will assemble in the servants hall, where tea, bread and butter, and buns will be distributed to them; two persons being appointed to hand around each of these things. After tea . . . the children will be taken up to the little drawing room, where a magic lantern will be exhibited to them. The presents for the children will have been previously arranged .

Forty-one children were expected but it is announced in the next issue that the expected event had to be cancelled: the whole of Whittingehame is blanketed in heavy snow, and trips on sledges drawn by two horses from the stables replace the anticipated entertainment. Happily, the next issue reports on the rescheduled party which was evidently a great success. After tea, "the children were taken up the stone stairs, across the corridor, through the library and in at the library door of the drawing room. As soon as they were seated the cap was removed from the magic lantern." The magic lantern show turns out to be replete with technical snags and a hair raising scenario is outlined. The oil lamp magic lantern having proved unsuccessful, an elaborate system of india rubber tubes from the gas lamp in the corridor had been rigged up but the lantern went out several times as the tubes detached themselves.

The third and final series of the *Whittinghame Advertiser* were produced for Christmas and New Year 1867-8. The newspaper is now quite sophisticated with a stencilled cover and the pages bound together. There is a direction that articles are to be placed in the Library let-

27 The magic lantern show: a Victorian engraving of a popular activity at Whittingehame.

ter-box by Thursday afternoons if intended for publication. A range of activities are reported on: riding, unsuccessful attempts at skating on the curling pond and skating pond due to insufficient ice, and the annual Farm Ball. On Christmas Day, in the Library, Lady Blanche read from *King Lear* and Handel's *Messiah* was performed by the the German governesses, the Misses Kling, and Miss Evelyn Balfour. The old year died to *God Save the Queen* and the New Year opened to *Hail Smiling Morn*.

The grass grows under nobody's feet in the New Year period. Dead birds are added to the Whittinghame Bird Museum at the House and on January 8 a Programme of Entertainment is mounted in the village schoolroom by Arthur Balfour, reader, and The Misses Kling, vocalists. The evening was orchestrated by A J B who read excerpts from Tennyson's *May Queen*, Adam Smith's *Wealth of Nations*, a chapter from *Pickwick Papers* and Macaulay's description of *The Siege of Londonderry*. Each of these worthy readings was prefaced by an introductory oration.

A successful shoot over the estate on January 10, in the company of invited guests, is recorded:

Pheasants	111
Hares	26
Rabits (sic.)	41
Woodcock	1
Partridge	1
Woodpigeon	1

This bag was achieved by brothers Arthur and Cecil, the Earl of Haddington (over from Tyninghame), Alexander Kinloch Esq (from Gilmerton House), T Mitchell Innes Esq, the Hon. J Nisbet Hamilton (from Winton House) and Henry Hope Esq.

The copies of the *Whittinghame Advertiser*[15] convey a delightful picture of an active, spirited and talented family which has successfully managed to create a remarkably self-sufficient world within the confines of Whittingehame. The close family interplay and confident sense of environment is to characterise the occupation of the House by the Balfours right up to the death of A J Balfour in 1930. That glorious sense of belonging imparted by Whittingehame was not just restricted to the family. In May 1868, Amalie Kling, one of the two sisters engaged as teachers for the children, wrote to Lady Blanche from Switzerland that their thoughts "wander back with great pleasure to Whittinghame which has become so very dear to us and especially to me who has found a second home there. I was made happy by its dear inhabitants. You can and will never know how how happy I often was."[16]

There were some other aspects of life at Whittinghame which demonstrated, at least to the outside world, that it was a country house which did not quite fit into regularly accepted patterns. During the American Civil War there was the Cotton Famine in Lancashire and not only did Lady Blanche subscribe to the fund for its relief, but she put an unusual proposal to the children. The staff establishment of the House was running below its usual level and she suggested that if they would undertake the work of the house then the money thus saved would go to the cotton workers of Lancashire. What those outside perceived as a quite extraordinary turn of events then took place. The house was divided and, according to Robertson, "The few servants remaining had the use of the stillroom at one end of it to prepare their own meals in and the kitchen was made over to Lady Blanche's daughters, who, after the two eldest had a few lessons from the cook before she left, did the family cooking." In this they were assisted, in the rougher work, by two "quite untrained" Lancashire girls brought from Manchester to stay at the House.

The sons were allotted duties normally handled by the male members of the downstairs household: polishing and cleaning knives, and the future Prime Minister was later to recall his vital contribution, "I helped to black the boots." Apparently, the meals at first were "irregularly achieved" and, on one occasion, the local minister was advised by Lady Blanche, "I would ask you to stay to luncheon, Mr Scott, but my daughters are doubtful if the steak will be rightly done !"[13] Doubtless, this distinctly unusual turn of events must have excited much comment at the time.

When Robertson took over from the Rev. Walter Scott, he was impressed by "her originality of thinking and of life" which "had its source in her great mental vigour". Robertson was presented to the parish in 1865 by Lady Blanche, acting as trustee and guardian of her eldest son. He describes how she would "talk long sometimes, walking backwards and forwards, perhaps, on the terrace that overlooked the lawn, on which her children might be playing croquet".[13] There can be little doubt that her strength of character and devotion to her children was crucial - especially in the formation of the character of young Arthur. As one writer observed, "In her breadth and her narrowness, in her absorption in her family, in her simple faith and imperious sense of duty, she recalls the gentle but spirited *chatelaines* of Thackeray."[8]

Lady Blanche certainly seems to have possessed a most remarkable ability to inspire loyalty and affection amongst those she employed. In 1901, her former ladysmaid (sic.), Margaret Duffield, wrote as an old lady to Alice Balfour of her deep and abiding affection for her former mistress and, rather more curiously, wrote that she "could not forget the most beautiful face I ever saw."[17] The extraordinary combination of humility and religious fervour of Lady Blanche, in which the mistress-servant relationship is firmly based on religious precepts after the fashion of the time, is shown in this portion of a prayer she wrote in 1851, at the age of just twenty-six:

> Teach me my duties to superiors, equals and inferiors. Give me gentleness and kindliness of manner and perfect tact; a thoughtful heart such as Thou lovest; leisure to care for the little things of others, and a habit of realising in my own mind their positions and feelings.

Give me grace to trust my children - with the peace that passeth all understanding - to Thy love and care. Teach me to use my influence over each and all, especially children and servants, aright, that I may give account of this, as well as of every other talent, with joy - and especially that I may guide with the love and wisdom which are far above the religious education of my children.

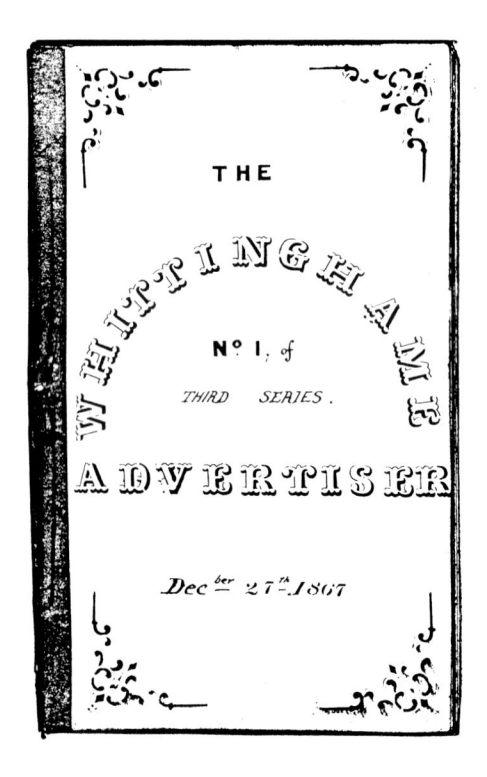

28 The cover of *The Whittinghame Advertiser*, 1867.

"A whirlpool of everything in life"

When Lady Blanche died in 1872, at the early age of 47 years, she was interred in the family cemetery in the grounds of the House. Within the next decade, unexpected tragedy was to strike the Balfour household twice again. Two of Arthur's brothers were to die at comparatively early ages. The second son, Cecil, a drunk, was to die in Australia in 1881 after falling from his horse. He had gone there under something of a cloud, if not as the black sheep of the family, having forged a cheque with Arthur's name. The third son, Francis Maitland Balfour, known as Frank, died climbing on Aiguille de Penteret, on the Italian side of Mont Blanc, in Switzerland in June 1882.

A J Balfour had, in fact, assumed responsibility for running Whittingehame House, the estate and its twenty farms immediately upon achieving his majority on July 25 1869, although he had made his first speech to a gathering of the tenantry at the early age of twelve. At fourteen he had left his preparatory school for Eton, a difficult regime for a young bespectacled intellectual in the making. After Eton there was Trinity, Cambridge, where he gained a Second in Moral Science.

In the July of his Tripos year he came of age and at Whittingehame there were bonfires, church bells and all the other celebrations traditionally associated with the majority of a young laird. There was a dinner with an elaborate menu prepared by a French chef and two double magnums of claret presented at the birth of the young heir were drunk. There were formal speeches. Young Balfour replied to those of his uncles, Lord Salisbury and Charles Balfour of Newton Don, and the Reverend James Robertson responded for the Clergy, expressing his gratification for the fact that Mr Balfour was a member of the Church of Scotland (presumably in the light of the fact that so many members of the landowning classes at that time were Episcopalians).

Throughout his life, Balfour was to live at Whittingehame, during the summer and holiday periods and, when Parliament was in session, he generally stayed at his London residence at 4 Carlton Gardens, which he acquired in 1870, or, occasionally, at the Salisbury home at Hatfield House. When he took over the running of Whittingehame House it was a sober and lifeless place. His mother, Lady Blanche, had never enjoyed good health and was terminally ill. It was a long time since the great public rooms on the ground floor had been used on any sort of regular basis. But all this was to change quite rapidly as a new world opened up for the young A J Balfour. In July of 1870, he stayed at Hagley Hall in Worcestershire, a guest of his university friend and fellow music lover, Spencer Lyttelton.

29 A J Balfour's uncle, Robert Cecil, 3rd Marquess of Salisbury (by Phil May).

There came his introduction to the closely interwoven worlds of the Gladstone and Lyttelton families. Spencer Lyttelton was the fourth son of the fourth Baron Lyttelton, who had married Mary Glynne. Her sister, Catherine Glynne, had married W E Gladstone, at a joyous double wedding in 1839. As a result of these two simultaneous unions a network of seven Gladstone and twelve Lyttelton cousins came into being and it was into this circle that Balfour now found himself introduced. It was a circle with which he was to be closely involved through his life and which, in turn, was to lead directly to the establishment of the group known as 'The Souls'. At Hagley that first weekend he met Mary Gladstone, the third daughter of the Liberal leader, and Lavinia Lyttelton, both of whom were to become friends for life. Spencer's sister, May Lyttelton, was also there and the nascent relationship between her and Balfour is generally considered to have had a profound effect on his personal development.

It is widely considered that Balfour was captivated by this young, lively girl and it is often suggested that it was Balfour's firm intention to propose marriage. There is no direct evidence of this but Mary Gladstone's observations and correspondence sometimes suggest this view. The liaison, however, was not to be. Despite a certain easy charm with the fairer sex, Balfour never appeared to get to the point of proposing marriage and in January 1875, May Lyttelton was to contract typhoid fever and die some ten weeks later. The young Balfour was observed to be devastated.

But the house party in the summer of 1870 was a roaring success and the next month A J invited them all to Whittingehame. Mary Gladstone, later Mary Drew, recorded: "Big party - Gladstones, Lady Rayleigh, Strutts, Lord Aberdeen, Lord Polwarth, 4 brothers Balfour. With stupendous and unheard of energy we sang . . . and at 11.45 p.m. started off on a walk to the garden, guided about in total darkness by the four brothers, pushed up hills, supported down dales . . ."[18] There were games, picnics and much merriment and laughter. The House began to live again and the period 1870-74 at Whittingehame was marked by an energy and gaiety, but which came to an end with the death of May Lyttelton.

In an unpublished memoir of Arthur Balfour, dated September 1917, Mary Drew was to write of this period. "I have never again seen quite the same lightness of heart and freedom from worries as between the years 1870 and 1880, though much of his gaiety of heart has come back under the influence of his home circle." [16] Mary Gladstone was at Whittingehame with Balfour in the summer of 1871, autumn of 1872 and the summer of 1874, besides being in his company on house parties at Hatfield, Hawarden, Hagley and Strathconan (the Balfour estate in the Highlands).

In 1874 Balfour became M P for Hertford and he was launched upon his political career in the new Parliament of Disraeli. Initially, it was undistinguished and by the end of 1875 he had still not spoken in the House of Commons. When he made his maiden speech in the following year it was on the subject of Indian currency: it was a subject which appealed to his abstruse intellectual abilities and was suitably non-contentious for a first contribution. In 1878 he became private secretary to his uncle, Lord Salisbury.

In 1886, after ten years of fairly undistinguished service, Balfour was appointed to his first Government post, Secretary for Scotland, by his uncle Robert Cecil (Lord Salisbury), which piece of neat nepotism gave rise to the popular saying, "Bob's your uncle". The following year, he became Chief Secretary for Ireland. This was not only a post with very considerable potential but, as ever, replete with dangers. To the alarm of the rest of the family, A J now carried a revolver on his tours of House and estate and two Scotland Yard detectives stalked him wherever he went lest Irish terrorists made their appearance ! This tended to irritate Balfour who took pleasure in giving his guards the slip, often sneaking out of the house by the side door, mashie in hand, to practise his golf swing while the detectives lurked unsuspectingly at the front door. His sister Alice complained that all they were concerned with was making amorous advances to the maids - on top of which they allegedly ate more than all the footmen put together !

In the early 1880s, the social whirl which had marked life at Whittingehame was replaced by an essentially family atmosphere in which A J Balfour, as head of the household, was surrounded by his brothers and sisters and a multitude of nieces. The whole household "revolved like the solar system around the sun, worshipping him with an unveiled idolatry of which he seemed to be sublimely unconscious," according to Lady Elcho. As a result of the political connections, the House was regularly visited by many of the politicians and intellectuals of the day. It became a regular meeting place of the group known as The Souls, which grew out of the Lyttelton-Gladstone connections.

Mary Gladstone seemed to have had mixed feelings about the widening of their social circle to include so many new people. "In 1884, Laura Tennant appeared on

30 A Victorian view of leisured life on the croquet lawn.

31 *Overleaf*: Croquet on the lower lawn, *circa* 1869. Note the conservatory, demolished in the renovations of 1871.

the scene. With Margot and the Ribblesdales, she simply romped in, drawing after her half the Stars of the Firmament. The atmosphere they brought with them was an atmosphere of rampant impulsiveness, bordering on recklessness, or more accurately 'headlongness' (a word used

55

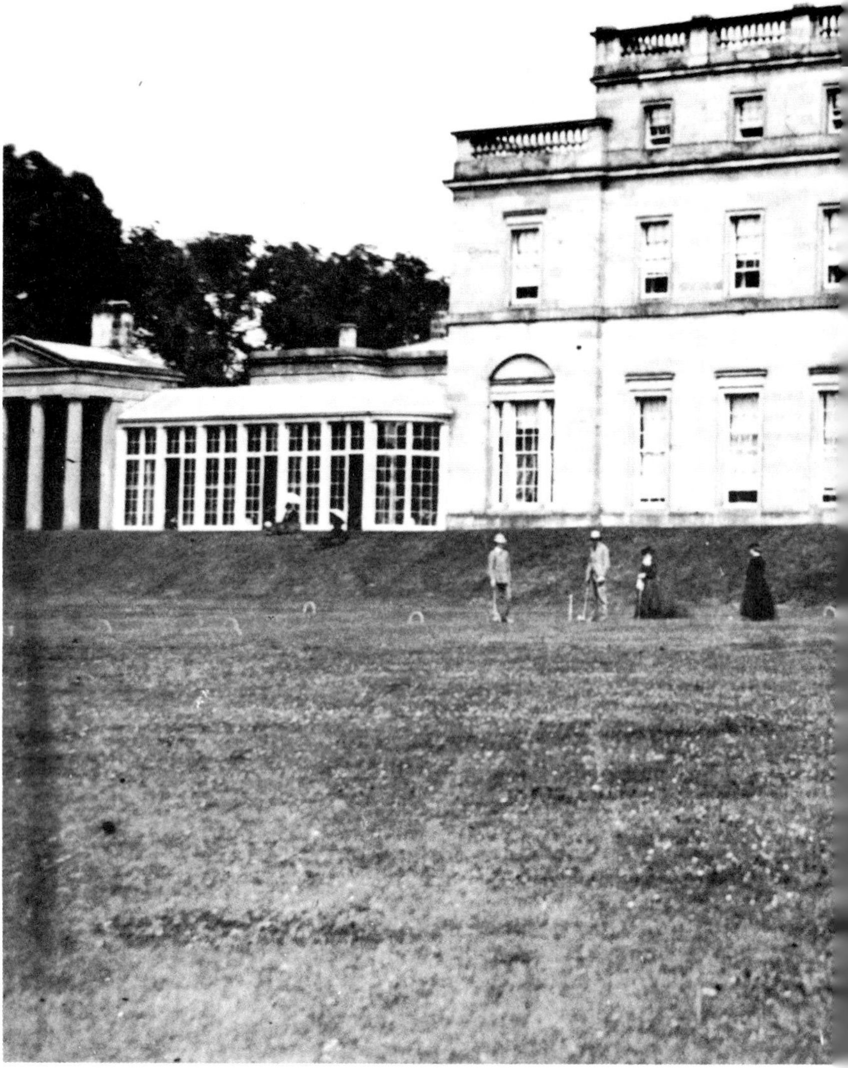

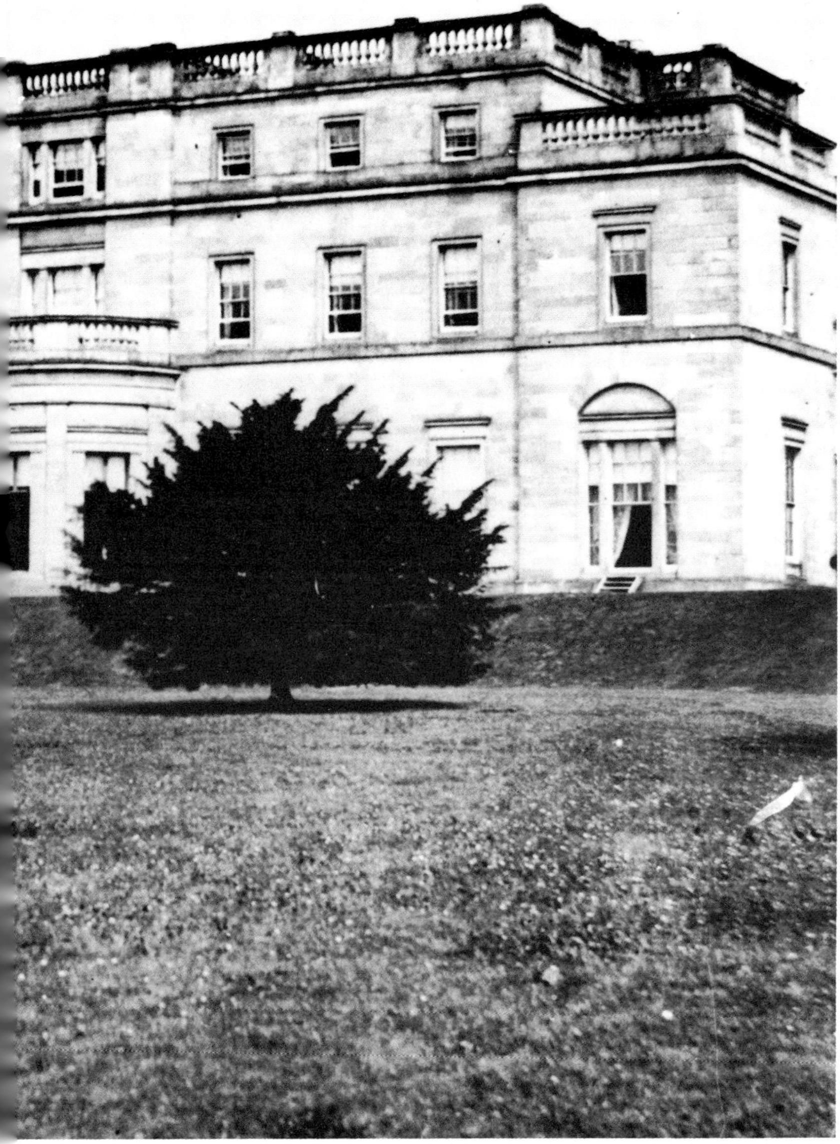

by a friend of Margot's). Constant introspection, constant criticism and competition, constant advertisement of its results, a passion for repartee, for scoring, for being a success, together with brilliant mental gifts, amazing power of insight, most genuine intellectual hunger, next to no serious flirtation or ill nature, and generally much warmth and generosity of heart." This must be one of the best, concise descriptions of The Souls ever made. [19] This dilettante group of aristocratic intellectuals, scathingly characterised by another contemporary writer as being less interested in Burke than *Burke's Peerage*, lent a sparkle and excitement to whichever country seat they graced. Lord Curzon, Lady Desborough, the Wyndhams and the Tennants formed the nucleus of the bright and witty circle. Apparently, "their conversation was generally as amusing as the games they were always ready to play after tea," according to a seasoned young observer.[17] Impersonations, paper games and a version of *Animal, Vegetable or Mineral?*, known as *Clumps* were all enthusiastically played. Not all games were so approved. On one occasion, Lord Elcho, then the M P for Haddingtonshire, introduced backgammon to nine-year-old Blanche Balfour one Sunday morning while the rest of the household was at church. This was not, however, welcomed and the 'winnings' were confiscated as "the wages of sin".[20]

A J Balfour was clearly still regarded as a highly eligible young bachelor with a romantic future. Eleven years after the death of May Lyttelton, Laura Tennant was herself to die in equally tragic circumstances of fatal illness. Her will, made in February 1886, left to Arthur Balfour - "my dear, deeply loved friend" - volumes of Shelley and Johnson and, revealingly, provided that "if he marries I should like him to give his wife my little red enamel harp - I shall never see her if I die now, but I have so often created her in the Islands of my imagination - and as a Queen has she reigned there, so that I feel in the spirit we are in some measure related by some mystic tie."[7] Balfour's various modern biographers have spent much time endeavouring to uncover the secrets of his private life. For Ruddock MacKay, Balfour was a "hermaphrodite", largely disinterested so far as the opposite sex were concerned. This rather curious conclusion is contradicted by the complete absence of any evidence of homosexuality (despite the nickname 'Pretty Fanny' applied to him early in his career),and by Kenneth Young who, quite to the contrary, discerns a long and "well documented", intimate affair with Lady Elcho, who lived not far away at Gosford House. Correspondence appears to suggest the start of this affair around 1885 with it cooling in ardour by 1900.

There were other lady friends with suggestions of a liaison with Etty, Lady Desborough, one of the pillars of the Souls. It is quite certain that the man who wrote "I would as soon marry a woman who was never interesting except when she was in a passion" was deeply interested in and fascinated by women. It is also possible that the intellectual and philosopher in him militated against actually getting to grips with an ostensibly irrational commitment to one woman.

Early political visitors at various times included Lord Salisbury, who was a regular visitor as A J's uncle, and William Ewart Gladstone, who became a friend in the 1870s following A J's introduction to the Gladstones at Hagley and who noted in his diary, apparently hopefully, following the first visit to Whittingehame: "How eminently he is *miglior luto* (of a finer clay) and how glad should we be to be nearer to him." [19] Winston Churchill, Lloyd George, Andrew Bonar Law and Joseph Chamberlain came later. The thinkers and the intellectuals of the day were represented by luminaries like A C Benson, Sidney and Beatrice Webb, H G Wells and Arthur Conan Doyle. Despite the frequent presence of visitors, apart from the welcome visits by the Souls, they were but tolerated and rarely managed to penetrate the tight family circle at the House.

"Visitors came and went at their own proposing, always received with groans, as disturbing to the large fam-

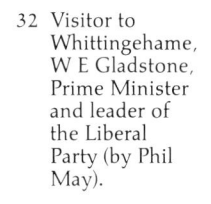

32 Visitor to Whittingehame, W E Gladstone, Prime Minister and leader of the Liberal Party (by Phil May).

ily circle, but very often enhancing its attractions. Sometimes an outsider would complain that Arthur was too much the centre of family life and thought. That all conversation was directed to make him talk, and that no one was considered worth listening to when he spoke. Nor were they . . ."[21]

Although the great noisy and sparkling house parties of the 1870s were never to be replayed, there were many guests and a range of both regular and special events as social form demanded. A J's sister, Alice Balfour, meticulously kept a book of Household and Entertainment Notes from 1894 up to 1920, recording numbers of invitations, guests and all the various costs involved.[22] The Christmas Treat for local schoolchildren and the Sunday school was a regular occurrence, together with tea and entertainment for all the families at the lodges and on the farms. These were quite extensive undertakings: in 1894, 121 people were invited and 90 actually attended. After tea in the servants' hall at 6.30 there were *Tableaux Vivants* enacted on a stage set up in the dining room. The acting, by the children of the House supplemented by the minister's nieces and factor's grandchildren, lasted more than one and a half hours with playlets based upon nursery rhymes, fairy stories and historical scenes. The expenses came to 18s. for the hire of 100 cups, plates and saucers and £1/7s for bread. A few days later there was a Childrens' Dance held in the dining room for the children of the House.

By the end of the century, the cinematograph was being introduced into parties for children and servants and was obviously a popular entertainment, for it was hired every year up to 1920. The operator was usually hired for the two performances and for many years James Buncle of Shandwick Place, Edinburgh - "everything can be easily fitted up in 1 hour" - was hired although by 1920 Lizars had taken over the provision of the entertainment. By the end of the War, the showing of films has clearly become a more complex undertaking: the Chief Constable is informed before each performance, the insurance company is advised and a copy of the Cinematograph Regulations Scotland of 1910 has appeared in the entertainments book.

The invitation lists for some of these entertainments are interesting for another reason. Many of them give an indication of the size of the establishment at Whittingehame. Invited to the Servants' Dance of 1900, in rough order of precedence are the following ladies: housekeeper, ladysmaid, cook, three housemaids, three kitchenmaids, two stillroom maids, three laundry maids, two nurses, two nursery and schoolroom maids, and two more ladiesmaids. There appear to be fewer men: the butler, valet, three inside men, four stablemen, and keepers and gardeners to make up the numbers.

The observance of special Royal occasions invariably brought celebrations to Whittingehame. On September 14 1911, there was a school treat in celebration of the Coronation of King George V. After buns and lemonade in the back yard of the House, there were sports on the lawns and terrace, including egg and spoon races, a tug of war, human wheelbarrow, three-legged and obstacle races. At the end, every child was given a Coronation mug. That week every woman householder on the estate received a photograph of the King and Queen and the especially favoured received Coronation numbers of the *Illustrated London News*.

But by far the greatest celebration ever held at Whittingehame was in August 1897 for the Diamond Jubilee of Her Majesty Queen Victoria. On the night of August 30, 500 estate workers were entertained at the Home Farm and, at the end of the evening of drinking, eating and dancing, Brock & Co., pyrotechnists of London, mounted a breathtaking firework display which culminated in a piece consisting of a crown and the words 'God Bless Her 1837-1897'.

The following afternoon there was the biggest garden party ever seen at the House. Alice's detailed notes record that 500 invitations were ordered - cost 12s.9d - and that of 355 sent out, covering around 850 persons, 530 actually attended. With typical thoroughness, she carefully considered and listed all those to be invited. It constitutes an interesting indication of the social pecking order:

1	All County families
2	All tenants of County places
3	Residents in or near North Berwick, Dunbar, Haddington and Linton to whom it would be advisable "to show civility"
4	Summer visitors
5	Edinburgh people
6	Tenant farmers on the Balfour estate
7	Ministers and clergy
8	Factors and agents of the large estates
9	Provosts, Bailies and Town Clerks of Dunbar, Haddington and North Berwick
10	Provosts of Police Burghs: East Linton, Tranent, Prestonpans, Cockenzie
11	County officials
12	Unionist agents

13	All doctors in the county
14	All bankers in the county
15	Other prominent men (but not tradesmen or working men)
16	Schoolmasters of parishes in which Mr Balfour has property
17	Ladies on the Hiring Friday Committee
18	All professors of Edinburgh University
19	All county councillors

Some fascinating and caustic notes are added to the subsequent record of arrangements. All did not go well in Alice's view. For instance the 55 by 30 foot tent, supplied by Binnie of Haddington for £4/10s, and which was put up on the lower terrace is recorded thus: "Note: When hiring a tent ascertain if it is clean."

A band consisting of 27 men from the Leith Volunteers, in bright scarlet uniforms, plus three professional musicians were engaged at a cost of £14 and £3/3s respectively. "Note: If a brass band plays indoors care must be taken to preserve the carpets as the men spit and empty their instruments all around."

There was some chaos attending the organisation of horses and carriages. "Police were engaged to marshall carriages, but as neither they nor the coachmen knew either how to arrange or obey, they were useless."

Alice's disapproval was not restricted to the hired hands. The guests were first received in the music room by herself and Arthur and a special temporary arrangement of steps down from the windows of both drawing room and library had been constructed to ease their flow onto the terrace. Alice noted "most people congregated obstinately just in front of the bow window steps . . . ." *Plus ca change* !

All Alice's irritations notwithstanding, the event was a great success blessed by fine weather and a good turnout. Claret and champagne cup were served on the terrace and there were tables groaning with food in library and drawing room. Everybody who was anybody attended and, indeed, all the names of those attending were printed in the local paper, presumably for the edification of the uninvited. The newspaper reported the presence of no less than the Lord Mayor of London in a somewhat surprised tone - he was "in the ordinary walking garb of a country gentleman". Including the mutton pies for the band and 6s for the useless help in the stables, the cost of the whole afternoon came to £48/13s.

The period of the Premiership after 1902 brought a rash of distinguished visitors to Whittingehame. King Edward VII planted an oak tree in commemoration of his visit and inspected House and grounds for half-an-hour. Joseph Chamberlain came in the autumn of 1901. "I did not think him agreeable company, nor did he put the company at ease wherever he was. This was due partly to his conversation being mostly about himself and his doings . . . ." Also, he played no games which was regarded as being decidedly poor form at Whittingehame, and so Balfour took him on long walks through the policies. At the end of his stay he did let slip that he was astonished at the extent of the grounds and that he had expected to find simply "a large house in a garden". This greatly tickled Balfour.[21]

Admiral Lord Kitchener, who visited in September 1902, also failed to favourably impress the experienced and critical occupants of Whittingehame. As a social asset he was something of a non-event: self-conscious silences blanketed the dinner table. "He early announced that he did not intend to go to our Church, as he did not like being stared at." He failed to realise that the the parishioners of the area were "quite conversant with men as great and more humble minded than himself."[21]

Later political visitors, during the General Election of October 1922, were Lloyd George, Lord Birkenhead and Sir Robert Horne. Political fortunes - and current misfortunes - were discussed animatedly over dinner, Joan noting "the disappearance of many glasses of brandy down Lord Birkenhead's throat." Everybody evidently enjoyed their evening and "dinner lasted until 10.30 - even Auntie (Alice) enduring black cigar smoke." On the Sunday morning, they all went to the small church at Whittingehame "through clicking cameras and crowds in the churchyard". The success of the weekend was made clear by the reaction of one of the guests. As he left the next morning, Sir Robert Horne observed of Balfour that "taking it all round he was the most distinguished figure in the world."[23]

At the end of that year, the new Prime Minister, Andrew Bonar Law, visited Whittingehame on his way to Glasgow. Balfour's fellow Scot was already a sick man, who was to die the following year, but the meeting went well with no embarrassment over Balfour's exclusion from the Cabinet. There was much talk of Balfour's work at the League of Nations and the rationale behind Law's removal of Lloyd George.

Many of these visitors expressed widely diverging views on the House. For Beatrice Webb it was "an unattractive mansion with large formal rooms and passages, elaborate furniture and heavy luxury totally without charm, somewhat cold in the fireless September phase. The atmosphere of gracious simplicity, warm welcome, intellectual interest, is all the more strikingly personal to the family that inhabits it."[24]

In fact, the first visit of the Webbs in September 1906, whilst on a tour of Britain to study the history of local government, was adjudged a great success by the Balfours who greatly admired them for their prodigious energy and their conversation. Over dinner they outlined their view of a Britain of the future divided into 'A's and 'B's: on the one side, Aristocrats, Artists and Anarchists ranged against, on the other, the Bourgeois, Bureaucrats and Benevolents. They classed themselves with the 'B's. According to Lady Betty, Gerald and Arthur were "sympathetic and interested". The innately aristocratic Frances felt "admiring hostility and boredom". And "Us Four (nieces were) extremely hostile because they interrupted *their* intercourse with 'Nunky'."[25]

The Webbs' view of a rather cold, cheerless house is, surprisingly, foreshadowed by Lady Frances Balfour in January 1880, although she was to warm to the place over the years as she spent more time there. "The cold of the house I remember vividly, it was warmed by a gas stove at the west end of the corridor concealed in an urn shaped ornament. This for economy was seldom lighted, and had not much effect when it was; the windows of the bedrooms did not fit; and the temperature of all the rooms was more often 50 degrees than near 60."[21]

Invited for lunch, A C Benson approached the House by bicycle in August 1904 (almost being summarily dismissed by the lodgekeeper at the west entrance) and was agreeably surprised: "We rode a long way in a richly wooded valley with steep braes and a stream - a noble approach; and finally arrived at the house. The whole thing surprised me by its opulence and magnificence. It is a very big, imposing house of grey stone; and the whole place trim, groomed, splendidly kept with an air of great wealth lavishly used."[26]

Balfour's biographer and niece Blanche Balfour (later Mrs Edgar Dugdale), daughter of Lady Frances and Eustace Balfour, and known within the family circle as 'Baffy', records that before the First World War the House was "a whirlpool of everything in life" with house parties and adults and children playing croquet and miniature golf on the lawns.[27] During this period three families effectively occupied the House simultaneously: A J Balfour and his sister, Alice; his brother Eustace married to Lady Frances Balfour (formerly Lady Frances Campbell) and

33 Joseph Chamberlain and A J Balfour caricatured in *Punch* (1903). The drawing admirably captures Balfour's langourous style. Chamberlain visited Whittingehame around this time but was reckoned to be a very dull house guest.

DURING THE INTERVAL.

Right Hon. J. Ch-mb-rl-n. "I SAY, ARTHUR, DON'T YOU THINK WE MIGHT DECLARE OUR INNINGS CLOSED NOW?"

Right Hon. Arth-r B-lf-r. "OH, FIELDING'S SUCH A BORE. LET'S LOSE A FEW MORE WICKETS FIRST!"

["It is rumoured that Mr. Chamberlain is in favour of an early dissolution."—*Daily Paper.*]

their family; and Gerald who was married to Lady Betty Lytton, daughter of the 1st Earl of Lytton, and family.

They all lived in the House with their families for six months of the year, from July to January. At other times of the year the great House was silent, blinds drawn and a reduced staff in residence. With the family away, there began in January the great annual cleaning of the house: picture rails, ledges, curtains and blinds all had to be cleaned and refurbished. The yellow brocade in the drawing rooms had to be brushed with soft brushes and rubbed over with tissue paper and soft silk dusters. Old polish was stripped from the furniture and new layers painstakingly built up. Wooden floors received similar treatment.

These two families of Balfour's nieces and nephews eventually numbered eleven, eight of them girls. The periods when A J was in residence were much looked forward to by his young nieces. "He was the most important person in our lives," Lady Eve Balfour remembered later, "Everything was fun if he was involved." For A J, the bachelor, it would seem that all these children about the house acted as something of a substitute for the family he never had himself and he was the centre of attention, the perfect uncle, 'Nunky' as he was known, at all times.

There were games, indoors and outdoors, and picnics on the beach with a procession of wagonettes and pony carts brought to the door to transport the adults and children to Tyninghame beach. Once at the beach, A J "strolled about, surrounded by an ecstatic giggling bodyguard of nieces."

For children in the 1880s, Whittingehame, with its many staircases and long corridors, was a place of excitement and adventure: "The nursery wing at Whittingehame opened on two staircases, leading down to the two separate worlds which make up the life of a great country house. The children of the family are the only members of the community who really have the freedom of both," wrote Blanche Balfour.

"On the first morning at Whittingehame, my first visit was always to the housekeeper's room. Down the stone stairs, along the stone-flagged passage, smelling of paraffin and boot-polish, where whistling footmen in shirtsleeves popped across. On through the swing-door which shut off the still-room and the store-room, a region scented with oranges and oatcakes on the girdle." In the housekeeper's room there was to be found the long-serving and faithful Mrs Anderson - or 'Fairy' as she was known to the children on account of her apparent magical qualities. "She was a little old woman, with a bony Scotch face, and deep-sunk blue eyes guarded by steel-rimmed spectacles. She wore a lace cap, and a woollen shawl pinned tightly over her thin shoulders with a large mother-of pearl brooch."[20]

Blanche Balfour writes vividly and fondly of the Whittingehame summers, from the excitement of arrival by means of the Flying Scotsman to Berwick upon Tweed and, from there, the slow train for East Linton. "In the station yard stood the Whittingehame carriages, old Sailor harnessed in the wagonette, and for us the brougham, with 'Mr Brett' himself on the box, and a pair of horses pawing the ground." Half an hour's ride then brought adults and children to the House where there were often the names of new servants to be mastered. There were always new young recruits and occasionally older ones were obliged to depart. The butler, for example, one morning began to beat the luncheon gong at eleven for no apparent reason at all "until all the grown-ups came out into the corridor." Within the hour the dog-cart, fit-

34 Day trip to the beach near Tyninghame: Alison, Joan, Nellie, Ruth and Gerald, 1906.

tingly enough, was ordered to take the hapless fellow and all his luggage away ! But, by and large, it was a closely regulated world founded on the two principles of "knowing one's work" and "knowing one's place".

35 Mrs Helen Anderson, housekeeper from 1875, taken in 1903.

The household was clearly an enlightened one. "The axiom that children should be seen and not heard did not prevail at Whittingehame. Anyone, however young, who had something to say was naturally expected to say it, and only if it was really silly was it discouragingly received. The profound respect for the individual which is characteristic of both Cecils and their Balfour cousins began early, and was the very foundation of social intercourse."[20] Formal meals were the only occasions when the caprices of children were indulged a little less: as Arthur Benson noted on his visit, "A pack of nice children had lunch at a separate table and were very quiet."[26]

There were certain regular rituals. On Sunday nights, once the dinner table was cleared, the bell would be rung in the courtyard and, a few minutes later, the gong sounded in the corridor. At this juncture after-dinner conversation in the library ceased and everyone returned to the dining room for worship. The gas lamps were turned down low and the red and gold curtains were closed. "Round two sides of the room stood the servants, more than twenty of them, white caps and aprons glimmering in the half light, and Fairy, in her black silk Sunday gown, at the end of the row of capless ladies' maids. At the other end was Mr Baker heading the line of menservants. When we had walked in and taken our places, they all sat down with one movement." At this point, A J Balfour would read from the Bible and there were prayers. Only ten minutes in duration, in many respects this was the focal point of the week, especially for the devout among the servants.[20]

On the last night of the year, all the children were allowed to see in the New. The family drank mulled claret and went to the front door of the House which A J opened to let in the New Year. On January 1 1892, Frances wrote to Betty about the New Year's Day celebrations. "I must tell you about New Years Day. It has been so Balfourian." There were presents for the children on the dining room table: masks, crackers, a tea set and carpenters' tools. Uncle Arthur put on a fox's head to the delight of the children and Gerald wore an elephant's head. Then there were games, Arthur having retired to his study, of snap-dragon, Animal Grab, Pounce and Old Maid. But by January 4 the bonhommie appears to have evaporated. "Saturday was a day of severe family squabbles, all ending peacefully but violent while they lasted." By January 9, as was the custom, the household is packing up after the Christmas and New year holiday and the carriages are loaded in bright sunshine and deep snow for the beginning of the long journey to London.[28]

36 The main hall with its Saucer-domed ceiling

"Disappointment when you are dealing with builders..."

In spring of 1871, A J had instituted the first of a series of 'renovations', for which he and his brother Eustace developed a passion, if not an obsession. For almost forty years - until money became a problem and a preoccupation - they were to be engaged in a constant process of change and renewal.

First of all, the terraces on the south side of the House were levelled down to allow more light and air into the basement area of the building. The existing conservatory was demolished. (Later, in 1896, Farquharson of Haddington was to add a glazed conservatory style corridor in glass and oak at the north-west end of the ground floor.)

Until 1872, the upper and lower terrace were simply divided by a grassy incline between the two levels. Stone balustrading was erected to encircle the terrace on the south side of the house; steps down to the lawns were constructed; the semi-circular bow window on the garden front was converted into a porch with *antae* in place of the original columns; and an elegant sundial holder of sandstone, with black marble supports, was erected on the new terrace. Carved in the sandstone were words from the newly fashionable 12th century poet Omar Khayyam's *Rubaiyat*:

> The Bird of Time has but
>
> a little way
>
> To fly - and Lo the Bird is on
>
> the Wing.

The dining room was remodelled in 1899 with a rich carved plaster ceiling and walls in grey, smoked Japanese oak by the craftsman Lawrence Turner, working under the direction of Eustace Balfour, who designed the ceiling himself. The carved oak panelling (the initials A J B were even worked into the shutters) and the richly ribbed and bracketed plaster ceiling created a room of opulence and period style "worthy of the guests and the conversation that the host, the best talker of his day, set going."⁸ A modern architect has estimated there to be no less than five tons of plaster in the ceiling ! Two carved sideboards were specially made from the same oak as used on the walls and new oak doors were fitted with what Lady Frances termed "fascinating" patent hinges.

A little later there was an interesting addition. An impressive enamelled overmantel by the designer and jeweller Alexander Fisher (1864-1936), after the style of the arts and crafts movement, intricately worked in bronze, ivory, enamels and semi-precious stones was exhibited at the New Gallery in London in 1900, purchased and brought to Whittingehame, where it was installed in the new dining room. This is reckoned to be one of the most

37 *Below*: The terrace created on A J Balfour's instructions, 1872.

38 The dining room prior to the remodelling of 1899. An arts and craft style side table had already appeared.

39 The ornate arts and crafts style overmantel by Alexander Fisher (1900) installed in the renovated dining room and reckoned to be one of the finest examples of the work of the arts and crafts movement.

73

important productions of the arts and crafts movement but it was, alas, stripped out and sold in the 1930s. It found its way to the United States but was retrieved in the early 1970s by the Fine Art Society who bought it at auction in New York, at that time unaware of its provenance, and returned it to Britain. Massive in its conception and dramatic in effect, it formed the centrepiece of their 1973 arts and crafts exhibition, found a new owner and for many years it has been on loan to the Victoria and Albert Museum.

New red and gold damask curtains were made and the Indian carpet was brought in from the library (it being replaced by a green carpet made in Donegal). The remodelling necessitated changes in the organisation of the pictures and the family portraits were relegated to the hall and stairs, together with the picture of Joseph and his children which had hung above the fireplace. The remodelling of the dining room, it is noted in A J's personal accounts for 1899-1900, cost a grand total of £1,171: a not insubstantial sum.

A little later, Eustace set to work on the drawing room and music room. Lady Frances reported to Lady Betty that he was "very childishly pleased with his yellow rooms. He has quite newly reopened the drawing rooms with yellow silk walls, and blue silk curtains." [29] In this choice of decor he was very much following the original scheme of James and Lady Eleanor Balfour but A J thought that the bright new yellow damask was "on the edge of being vulgar". He suggested to Alice that a soft green silk paper might be more suitable but, in the end of the day, they learned to live with the yellow. The Sevres

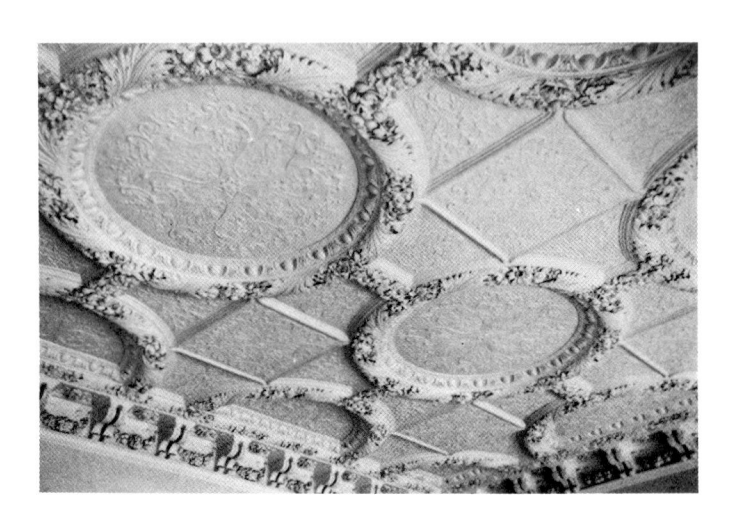

40 The richly moulded dining room ceiling by Eustace Balfour and Lawrence Turner (1899).

china acquired by The Nabob was still on display in the drawing room and a little later - in 1909 - new cabinets were ordered to house it.

Both A J and Eustace Balfour took an interest in the work of what were, for the time, distinctly modern and *avant garde* artists, and A J bought many works by members of the arts and crafts movement. Blanche Balfour writes of "my father's early devotion to the works of William Morris and Burne-Jones." Edward Burne-Jones (1833-1898) and his son, Philip Burne-Jones (1862- 1926), became firm friends of their patron. Blanche put it somewhat more strongly, "We adored 'Mr Phil'." Most of the Burne-Jones acquisitions remained at Carlton Gardens although some of the striking mythological scenes did find their way to Whittingehame. There was also a magnificent handprinted wallpaper featuring a peacock design, possibly drawing its inspiration from ancient designs featuring the peacock as the symbol of immortality. It was used in one of the first floor bedrooms and its dressing room and the design is thought to have been the work jointly of Edward Burne-Jones and William Morris (1834-1896), who printed the design at his London workshops. It bears some similarity to his well known woodpecker tapestry (1885).

During restoration work in 1989, the boarded up fireplace in what had been A J Balfour's study was opened up again to reveal some exquisite tile-work which has been identified as the work of artist, potter and writer William de Morgan (1839-1917). Latterly, in the late 1880s and early 1890s, Morris obtained his tiles exclusively from De Morgan's workshops for, according to the *Encyclopaedia Britannica* of the time, he had "perhaps made the greatest advances of all, having re-discovered the way to make and use the the beautiful thickly-glazed blues and greens of the old Persian ware."

A J Balfour was constantly searching for the works of new craftsmen and artists. On one occasion, he writes excitedly to Alice from London that he has found "a new landscape painter". Passing the Leicester Galleries by chance, he dropped in and bought, on the spot, five pictures by a young artist called Oliver Hill (1887-1968). The new pictures were to be brought to Scotland to join the Constables and de Konings on the Whittingehame walls. Curiously, these latter are disliked by Alice but she is assured, "If I can afford it I shall certainly buy, in the course of years, some good pictures, which would replace the second best . . ." One of the painters he is desirous of acquiring is Corot: "uniformly charming". And, in August

1890, he writes to Alice of being painted by Sir Lawrence Alma Tadema (1836-1912).

Additional servants' accommodation was built on the second floor by the creation of four attics. In Lady Blanche's day, comfort had not rated as a top priority but 1872 correspondence shows that Balfour gave early instructions for more modern methods of heating. Sibbalds of Edinburgh were instructed to instal heating equipment, piping, coils and boiler to heat the main hall, stairs and entrance hall, all for the cost of £172/10s., excluding cartage from East Linton railway station.[30]

There was installed in the basement on A J Balfour's instructions by Chubb & Son, safemakers from London, a large room lined in iron with heavy safe door put into use for the storage of cabinet papers, silver caskets containing borough freedoms, gold keys with which public buildings had been opened, silver trowels with which foundation stones had been laid and golf trophies. "Mr Balfour must often be at a loss to remember who the donors were, and when and where some of the gifts were showered upon him." [10]

Between 1900 and 1902 some rather more unfortunate changes were instituted by A J's architect brother, Eustace. The newly fashionable renovator of the Scottish country house, Sir Robert Lorimer (1864-1929), who had been a house guest at both Whittingehame and nearby Biel House, was engaged to help modernise certain aspects of the building. Most distressingly, he was involved with Eustace in the building of the urn-bearing excrescence which stands beneath Smirke's *porte-cochere*, which, although it was, admittedly, "threaded with fiendish ingenuity" [8], ruined the elegance of the north facade and served to introduce the present rather mean double-door front entrance. Family photographs taken in 1902 by Eustace Balfour show the occupants of the House standing before the infilled portico. Around the same time, astragals were removed from the ground floor windows on the south facade and replaced with plain plate glass. As Lady Frances observed, "Arthur Balfour . . . would never hear of Utility being subordinated to Preservation." Lorimer did design some interesting door handles, light switches and other ironmongery, cast by Henshaws, the architectural ironmongers in Edinburgh, a few of which do still survive at the front entrance to the House.

The infilling of the *porte cochere* meant that the entrance hall, in fact, now became an inner hall and it also came to serve as a billiard room. After the Great War, the flag of a German submarine captured off Le Havre hung on the fireplace wall flanked by swords and heraldic re-

41 Family and guests at the door of the House, September 1902. The only member of the house party not in the picture is Eustace Balfour: he was the photographer.

galia: coats of arms taken off enemy transport when the British advanced into Bulgaria, a sword from Mesopotamia and a similar trophy from Armenia. These trophies of war were supplemented by two white marble busts of General Bluecher and the Empress Marie Louise.

After 1906, following his election defeat, A J finds he has more time to enjoy Whittingehame and, inevitably, there are more improvements made to the property. A classical temple was erected near to the Tower in 1905, and in 1909 he is in correspondence with Eustace about further improvements to the balustrading and terrace. In 1915 the handsome wrought iron gates were installed at the entrance to the walled garden.

He was often impatient at the progress of renovations. In October 1909, he wrote to Alice in some anguish: "I cannot get over my emotions at the length of time the Whittingehame changes have taken. Disappointment when you are dealing with builders and building is no doubt the lot of man . . . " He took an interest in every tiny detail of arrangements at the House. "My own view is that portraits should not be hung in the drawing room. Most of ours are either copies or of no great artistic merit . . . the china and furniture in the drawing room are sufficiently good to make it worth while hanging there our best pictures . . . I am a little afraid of dwarfing the billiard room by placing in it any pictures disproportionately large . . . in any case there ought not to be *two* pictures of me in the drawing room." Family portraits were to be relegated to the stairs and less popular paintings to the corridors.[31]

In A J's frequent absences, his domestic affairs were looked after by his sister, Miss Alice Balfour. She was a redoubtable lady who was an intrepid traveller in southern Africa in the early 1890s - authoress of *Twelve Hundred Miles in a Waggon* - and she effectively ran the household. She did not marry, had a poor opinion of her own physical appearance and, apparently, was not over-fond of men as a species. She was frequently difficult and a very particular sort of person. Often jealous of her brother's friends, she failed to welcome them in the House. And she was at daggers drawn with Lady Frances Balfour, the wife of Eustace. Alice was a meticulous housekeeper and kept a close check on every tiny aspect of the running of the establishment, which included frequent inventories of household equipment and visits to the wine cellar to check the stock. She made clear her disapproval of unacceptable behaviour and personal peccadilloes. There was rarely enough wine at dinner and Eustace had a considerable capacity for it which occasioned regular argument over the provision of further supplies. Nevertheless, she was good with the tenants, the children and all animals and she was both a keen horticulturalist, responsible for adding the impressive 132-tree lime-tree avenue to the north of the House, and lepidopterist, presenting her complete collection of East Lothian butterflies to the Royal Scottish Museum in Edinburgh. A J clearly valued her abilities and her essential contribution to the life of the House: the fourth Earl of Balfour recalls that after the First War she had an annual dress allowance of £2,000.

During A J's incumbency there were also many practical improvements. At the stables, a gasometer was installed and, for a time, gas was supplied from the village of East Linton, three miles distant. Electricity was produced by a private generating plant and, in the late 1890s, running water had been introduced at the east and west ends of the building. In the first decade of the century five new bathrooms were created; during the works to create a bathroom at the east end of the building in 1987, masons' marks dated 1898 were discovered behind wood panelling. Water was supplied during the 1870s direct from a natural spring more than two miles away in the Lammermuir Hills by means of a cast-iron pipe. Hydrants were installed around the building against the eventuality of fire and, in the days before Edinburgh Fire Brigade enjoyed the benefit of motor transport, there were fire practices attended by every able-bodied man on the estate. The big bell in the kitchen court was violently rung and "cascades of maidservants issued from the mouth of the tubular fire escape fixed to a window of the upper storey, shrieking with fearful joy."[21] Hosepipes were connected to the hydrants by gardeners and foresters and were trained on the building, until they seemingly inevitably began to leak, which caused A J to subside into a state of deep gloom.

Another modern and entirely practical innovation in 1909 was the installation of a handsome, wood-panelled, electrically operated passenger lift at the west end of the building, connecting all four floors of the house. "The lift people are much pleased with the working of the engine," wrote A J in eager anticipation in the September. Doubtless, this might have made life easier for the servants but one suspects that it was installed rather out of A J's passion for anything new !

When Balfour took over the estate in 1869, the account books show that there were 12 gardeners headed by William Rintoul, who was paid £75 per annum "with fuel and light". There were also a dozen foresters to maintain the trees and the drives. Many handsome trees were introduced into the grounds, including copper beech, Scots pine, specimen lime and rhododendron bushes. A photograph taken in 1897 shows these last as knee-high bushes newly planted. Imported from Tibet, they were later cut in the shape of an anchor to commemorate A J Balfour's period as First Lord of the Admiralty in the coalition government of the First World War. Potted yews were added on the terrace. A unique *eucalyptus Whittingehamensis*, was brought to Britain from Australia as a seed by Lord Salisbury in 1846 and was planted across the glen. Somewhat surprisingly, it established itself in the somewhat indifferent climate and flourished for many years: in 1893, the *Ordnance Gazetteer for Scotland* noted that it was 53 feet high and over eight feet in girth at a foot above the ground. In 1902, it is recorded, there were no less than 40 acres of lawns and eleven miles of paths and drives in the grounds of the House. It is said that Balfour knew virtually every tree upon the estate and he was particularly interested in experiments in the growth of hardwood trees.

Another change worth noting was brought about at the instigation of Alice Balfour. The spelling of the name of the House and the village, previously known as Whittinghame or Whittingham, now became Whittingehame - the middle syllable of the name being pronounced, as a contemporary observer put it, "as when a bracing breeze brings a *tinge* of colour to the face." By all accounts, she had tired of the idle pronunciations of "Whittenham" which had come into use - even in the local school - and resolved to institute a change. A limerick was even devised to highlight the new pronunciation.

> There was an old person of Whittingehame
> Who was forced by fate to sit in a jam,
> When her friends cried "Alas",
> She but said "Let that pass",
> This collected old person of Whittingehame.

42 The Upper Library, November 1904.

On June 16 1897, Her Majesty's Postmaster General wrote to Alice: "I am glad to inform you that it has now been arranged for the name of Whittingehame to be so spelt in official publications, so that I trust your wishes in this respect will be complied with." [31] Alice also conducted correspondence with the Inspector of Ordnance Survey in Edinburgh to ensure that her changed spelling might become generally accepted and recognised. "Quite useless," opined Lady Frances Balfour, "I mean to stick to the old spelling !"[21] The views of Lady Frances were most probably influenced by the acrimony which existed between her and Alice. On another occasion, Alice observed to A J that she intended to change the name of one of the bedrooms to accommodate its new wallpaper. Lady Frances was moved to expostulate across the dining table, "Can you believe that anyone except a perfect fool would change the name of a room because they changed the paper ?"

A J Balfour sometimes found it difficult to adapt to some of the rigours of country life. For light reading he was fond latterly of P G Wodehouse and it is, perhaps, no coincidence that he dreaded, just like Lord Emsworth of Blandings Castle, the incursions of uninvited guests and the general public "when a tidal wave of the peasantry and its squealing young engulfed those haunts of immemorial peace".[32] According to Lady Frances, "They marked the approach of gentle or simple to their house or policies with complete horror." A J used the terminology of Mark Twain to describe incursors as "tramps and bounders."

"On the approach of 'carriage company', if they were engaged out of doors in playing croquet or lawn tennis, they would run with great dignity, and equal agility within the sheltering arms of a lime tree which at that time, swept its covering boughs over these inhospitable inmates. There they imagined they were invisible. From their covert they would emerge when the danger of seeing a neighbour was over, and highly amused at the success of their strategem."[21] This behaviour initially appeared rather strange to Lady Frances, who, as Lady Frances Campbell, had been accustomed to the accessibility of the estate at Inverary Castle where large numbers of people came and went more or less as they wished.

One gains an impression of elaborate game playing; of a private joke practised against the outside world; of a world of carefully cultivated intellectual rather than social snobbery. Beatrice Webb perceptively divined this attitude during her second visit in the autumn of 1910: "There is a delightful atmosphere of intimacy . . . it is gained at the expense of aloofness from the world, from the countryside, from the world of experts and administrators, even from the world of Conservative politicians."[24]

This same view of the rest of the world is echoed by Mary Drew. "I remember asking A J B if he was aware that the whole population of the world, roughly speaking, could stand on the Isle of Wight with a square yard to each person . . . Mr Balfour's answer was highly characteristic. 'I wish to Heaven they all were.'"[19]

The intellectual capacity for clarity of thought and the application of logic was a much appreciated attribute by those living within the confines of the House. On one occasion, Alice arrived from Dunbar railway station having been involved in a railway accident, such occurrences being a fairly regular feature of the Edwardian period. She was immediately quizzed about all her actions during the course of the incident but once the questioners had established the fact that she behaved in a logical manner under stress, all discussion of the matter ceased. Another time, an empty canoe was discovered down at the Water, Balfour's brother Frank having evinced his intention to go canoeing. There was clearly a *prima facie* case to consider that he had drowned. To the surprise of Lady Frances, the family sat around and debated the matter and she noted "with astonishment the cool calculation of the family that the probabilities were all in favour of his being safe. And so it turned out."

In 1903, Balfour was invited to become an Honorary Member of The Speculative Society of Edinburgh and the logical thinker and philosopher was much pleased to be enrolled as a member of what was, and is, not only the exclusive pinnacle of intellectual life in Scotland's capital city, but also believed to be the oldest debating society of its kind in the world.

There were, however, a few occasions when even A J Balfour could not protect himself from the rough and tumble of the world outside the House and grounds at Whittingehame. He harboured a very real fear of the annual dance for estate workers held after Christmas in the barn at the Home Farm. A J was for hours beforehand plunged into a black gloom known as the 'Farm Ball mood', recalling J M Barrie's line in *The Admirable Crichton*, "Even to think of entertaining the servants is so exhausting."

As he dreaded the party, he also disliked the traditional country pursuits of hunting and shooting. He wrote to Edward Talbot, Bishop of Rochester who had married Lavinia Lyttelton, about life at Whittingehame in

January 1878: "You ask for news of what we have been doing at Whittingehame: but I will not drag you through the details of that painful three days which is annually given up to the horrors of the shooting party. Since that scourge has been withdrawn, I have been left in tolerable peace."

He goes on to describe the days at the House: "Every man retires for a quarter part of the day to his respective den, emerging at meal times like a giant refreshed and prepared to argue at any length or any side of any question. To enumerate all the subjects which have been exhaustively discussed would be impossible. But I may mention among others, contemporary politics in all its branches, the theory and practice of shaving (this with great minuteness to Alice's disgust), a large number of mechanical and other scientific problems, wine (this with more energy than knowledge), Transcendental Philosophy, Art, and the London Markets - price of copper and so forth . . ."

We get the impression of something of a hive of intellectual activity: "At present this house is a 'Temple of Research'. Gerald and Cecil are not doing much but Frank, though he supposes himself to be taking a holiday, is I believe preparing his book for the press (in the smoking room), Eustace (in the billiard room) is drawing the illustrations for *his* book, Henry Sidgwick is finishing his article for the Encyclopaedia and writing a paper for the Metaphysical Society in *his* sitting room, while I, in mine, am working very hard . . .

"If I add to this that Alice is groaning over the iniquities of the house in her 'boudoir' while Cecil is reading through the City articles in the Library and Gerald strumming on the P.F. pianoforte in the drawing-room, I shall have exhausted both the party and the house . . . "

Argument, debate and intellectual activity of every type was the norm in this extraordinary household with its well-established routine. A J's two eldest sisters, Nora and Evelyn, had married eminent figures in their fields: Henry Sidgwick, Fellow and Tutor of Moral Philosophy at Trinity, Cambridge, and Lord Rayleigh, physicist and discoverer of argon. Both fitted well into the regime of Whittingehame.

In the mornings A J would take his breakfast in bed in the large bedroom on the centre of the first floor with its commanding view down the newly planted lime tree avenue and out to the North Sea beyond. He would then dictate letters in his bedroom. There was lunch in the dining room with the family and any other visitors to the House and afterwards he retired to his study at the corner of the building on the ground floor to read and to write - and where he was interrupted only at the peril of the interloper. Blanche Dugdale recalls one such occasion when there was "an invasion of a young instalment of nieces, who, having cooked for him a sparrow rolled in clay according to Red Indian recipe, had presented it on a platter, and were seated round in hopes of seeing him eat it."[20] Balfour did not eat the offering but was, as usual, particularly indulgent of his young nieces. Later in the afternoon there might be some golf or tennis in the grounds with tea taken in the library. Of an evening there was dinner in the dining room and thereafter bridge, music or, perhaps, billiards, of which Balfour was fond. There were at various times two billiard rooms in the house: when the main entrance hall became an inner entrance hall after Lorimer's renovations, a table was placed there. Previously, billiards had been played in the ground floor room at the corner of the building, opening off the drawing room.

Books were a passion marked by lavish buying. A J was reckoned to possess one of the finest private libraries in Britain and the thousands of leather and cloth covered volumes were all stamped in gold with the legend 'A J Balfour, Whittinghame' or 'Whittinghame Library' together with an accession date. The vast library overflowed with volumes for which there was no available shelf space and his own study "was packed from floor to ceiling" and its sofas "were heaped with flotsam and jetsam of current publications." According to Blanche Dugdale, "the books at Whittingehame had an alert look about them, as if expecting to be pulled out at any moment." It usually fell to Lady Frances to endeavour to introduce some order to the library and the vast collection of books. Not only were they bought by A J, but often house guests gave a welcome present of books. In September 1906, Arthur Conan Doyle formally wrote to Alice at Whittingehame with his thanks for a pleasant stay - "if I could feel that I have diverted Mr Balfour's thoughts for one day I should feel my existence justified" - and sent his collected works to Lady Frances "in the hope that some niche may be found for it."[31]

The journalist R A Dakers wrote in 1905, after a visit to write about the home of the Prime Minister, "The atmosphere of Whittingehame is books. The walls are built of books." He had heard that, a few days before, the Prime Minister had a corner of his shelves cleared to make room for more books and two cartloads of ejected volumes had been sent to the library at Haddington. Apparently, "Every visit of the Premier brings more books."

He espied in the study, within reach of the Premier's outstretched hand, his favourite volumes: the works of Keats, Kipling and Robert Louis Stevenson.[33] Balfour was to be found wandering along corridors at all hours of the night and day, most likely in search of some mislaid volume. (At the very least, he had not taken up the habit of the 3rd Lord Wallscourt, who resided at Ardfry House in Co. Galway. He used to like walking around the house naked at the dead of night and his wife was obliged to persuade him to wear a cowbell so as to warn the maidservants of his approach.) Most of Balfour's library was dispersed in the 1930's although, to this day, odd copies turn up in secondhand bookshops and at auction.

The summer days at Whittingehame allowed the man of state to unwind and relax with the things he enjoyed most. Balfour was not so much interested in the conventional country pursuits - fishing, shooting, hunting and so on - but rather served to popularise some rather unfashionable sports: specifically, golf and cycling.

Every summer between 1891 and 1914 he would remove himself the few miles to nearby North Berwick and spend a month playing golf, which he had enthusiastical-

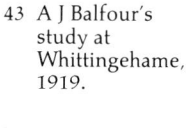

43 A J Balfour's study at Whittingehame, 1919.

ly embraced from 1886, staying in a hotel overlooking the 17th green and the first tee, returning to Whittingehame on Friday evenings for the weekend with the others. He would play two rounds a day, laying aside the evenings for his writing and political work. "Golf," he said, "has all the thrilling excitement of deerstalking without its inconveniences and dangers." And, writing on 'The Humours of Golf'in the Golf volume in The Badminton Library of Sports and Pastime, he rather revealingly observes, "Care may sit behind the horseman, she never presumes to walk with the caddie." His newly found passion for golf led to the creation in 1888 of a small seven hole golf course on the terrace and lawns to the south of the House. Lady Frances drily noted that "it will save it from being made a flower garden".[34] A J himself later commented, possibly a little defensively, that the course had been laid out "chiefly with a view to the enjoyment of the ladies of the house." For him, there were the more serious links at North Berwick and one suspects that he was never so happy as in those summer months when he played golf all day and wrote metaphysics all night.

44 The Library in 1919. A photograph taken for *The Scots Pictorial.*

It has been said that prior to Balfour s interest in cycling it was for "cads on castors" but, that notwithstanding, the outer hall at Whittingehame bore the twin-wheeled evidence of this preoccupation. On one occasion, in the 1890s, he turned up at the House of Commons with one arm in a sling and one foot in a slipper, the consequence of a collision with a carriage. Without a doubt he would have subscribed to the hymn of praise to the velocipede composed by his friend Arthur Benson, the Eton housemaster:[26]

> Praised by thou, O my Lord, of our brother the Bicycle,
>
> Who holdeth his breath when he runneth,
>
> And is very swift and cheerful and unwearied, and silent.
>
> He beareth us hither and thither very patiently,
>
> And when he is sick he doth not complain.

For a brief period in the late 1890s there was a passing fad for the motor tricycle and Balfour could be espied speeding along the lanes and roads in the vicinity of the House.

Croquet and tennis were far more conventional country house pursuits and they were enthusiastically played at Whittingehame. An early interest in real tennis gave way to lawn tennis when a court was prepared at the House. Indeed, Balfour played well beyond the age of 70. Asquith jealously observed him playing at Whittingehame as late as 1928. There was a hard court less than one hundred yards from the house, where A J perfected "a service and return extremely difficult to take owing to a spin which he gives the ball." The acres of lawns lent ample opportunity for croquet, the mallets and equipment finding a home in Smirke's Greek temple.

There was also provision for winter sports at Whittingehame. About one mile and a half to the west of the House, at Overfield, a curling pond was created and nearby there was also a skating pond. In the Christmas holidays the children would often clamber into a sleigh in which they were drawn across the estate by two horses from the stables. The winter of 1882 brought a new outdoor pursuit to Whittingehame: tobogganing. Toboggans, then uncommon in Britain, had been acquired in Canada and in December heavy snow brought "an early opportunity to use these ships of adventure." According to Lady Frances, "We all took vigorously to the sport, Arthur destroying a laburnum tree in the steepest part of the Glen, in order to get a peculiarly high and dangerous run."[21]

One summer, the regular sports activities were supplemented by the formation of a Whittingehame House hockey team, recruited from family and household, and on one occasion everyone went to play the nearby house at Nunraw. Balfour was asked by someone if he was to take part. "No," he replied, "but if all goes well I am here to crown the hall-boy with laurel."

Life at Whittingehame seems upon first examination to have been a perfect rural idyll in which all the participants pursued their private passions free and unfettered. One guest suspected, however, that all was not quite as it appeared. Cynthia Elcho, later Lady Cynthia Asquith, visited from nearby Gosford House where her mother lived. She thought "Arthur Balfour never shone quite so brightly in his own home as elsewhere ... my impression was that in some ways Arthur Balfour lived like a guest in his house." There can be little doubt that in this she was making a thinly veiled reference to the presence and influence of his sister, Alice, who was responsible for so many domestic eccentricities: clocks all ran one hour ahead of time, to ensure appointments were kept, the

45 Below left: A J Balfour on the links at North Berwick.

46 A cartoon satirising Balfour's preoccupations with golf and motoring.

ANOTHER CASE OF "FURIOUS DRIVING" AGAINST MR. B-LF-R.

numbers of spoons, forks and other cutlery was regularly checked, smoking was banned apart from in an unfriendly room set aside for that purpose and all communal activities restricted on Sundays.

A letter from London in the August of 1900 brought news to Whittingehame of the introduction of a considerable novelty: a four and a half horsepower De Dion Bouton *voiturette*, together with an engineer specially engaged to look after same. The De Dion was purchased by A J at a cost of £240 and superceded the motor tricycle which had been bought the previous year for £122. This primitive motor car was prone to stop suddenly, run backwards down steep hills, of which there are in abundance around Whittingehame, and fail to stop at speed. What caused it to break down "formed an inexhaustible and dreary topic of conversation, as tedious as the noise of an exhaust pipe." [21] The engineer was obliged to make a wedge which could be placed behind the rear wheels and prevent it from rolling backwards down hills. It ultimately came to an inglorious end at the hands of young Blanche Dugdale whilst she was transporting a distinguished visitor, the diplomat Sir Charles Eliot. The brake failed to work to any degree and Sir Charles was so discomfited he insisted on walking back to the House. "He gave Uncle Arthur so lurid an account of the dangers . . . that it was decided to discard the *voiturette* in favour of a real motor car with an efficient chauffeur." On another occasion, Sir Thomas Buxton missed his train at East Linton because the wretched car failed to start. Lady Frances quickly tired of the love affair with the motor car: "Arthur, to my horror, devastated the early part of dinner by motor shop . . . . He forecast the great roads for motorists alone, when speed would be without limit, and nothing but motors were allowed. They were to radiate from all parts of the country, and to find their centres in great cities . . . . I sat wondering when he would stop, his small audience charmed and amused."[35] Alice was also discomfited. She was concerned as to when the engineer, a man of voracious appetite, would depart.

In due course, a large new 40 h.p. Napier car arrived and Mills was engaged as chauffeur. Balfour became an early enthusiast for the modern motor car, exceeding the speed limit on many occasions when he drove himself. [11] The acquisition, nicknamed 'the Flyer,' was much admired. Balfour's passion for the motor car was much caricatured and sometimes clouded his judgement as he revealed with his mistaken observation, "The motor car will help to solve the problem of congestion of traffic." He had a number of cars, and he was often photographed at the front door of Whittingehame climbing into and seated in these conveyances. But it must have been a very special day on July 25 1928, the occasion of his 80th birthday, when both Houses of Parliament presented him with a Rolls-Royce motor car in recognition of his long service and many achievements.

No less a personage than King Edward VII expressed his admiration for the Napier. In September 1902, he was staying with the Saxe-Weimars in North Berwick and A J Balfour collected him in it and brought him to Whittingehame to visit the home of his Prime Minister. As was to be expected there was great excitement at the House - not least on account of the enforced abandonment of lessons - and the children gathered in the nursery to see the car approach the House by the west approach, with their Uncle Arthur and the King in the back, closely followed by the Chief Constable's car. The eight children were all then summoned to the library to meet the King, shaking hands and curtseying to the monarch and, with the introductions accomplished, "we all stood in a ring around him, all staring at him, till Aunt Frances pulled us to the back of the room," wrote 12 year-old Nellie Balfour to her mother Betty. His Majesty made a rapid tour of the dining room, drawing room and study, commented upon Eustace's renovations, planted his tree and went off again after twenty minutes or so.[36]

Another new-fangled invention appeared at Whittingehame in January 1906, following the election campaign in which the Balfour administration was defeated and the Conservatives routed. Arthur wrote defensively to Alice on December 30 1905 that "I am afraid you will think that I have added to the terrors of life at Whittingehame." He had bought something of which the children were to have "absolute use".[37] As the car drew up at the door the following week and the nieces descended upon it, an enormous gramophone trumpet of polished brass emerged from the car, borne by Uncle Arthur. Such objects were still considerable novelties and he was much pleased with his acquisition. The next day was spent in Edinburgh at Paterson's music shop in George Street, whence the family returned with the Napier laden down with everything from Handel and Beethoven (doubtless chosen by A J) to *Annie Laurie* and the *Choristers' Waltz*. "The brazen trumpet blared by night and by day through the long corridors of Whittingehame House for the rest of the brief holiday." Children and adults were united in their excitement at the new toy.[27]

47 The De Dion motor car in front of the house, 1900, with Blanche Balfour at the wheel.

48 The 40 h.p. Napier in front of the House with A J Balfour and Mills, the driver, in the front, behind Alison, Joan, Nellie and Ruth. Gerald Balfour standing beside the car, 1904.

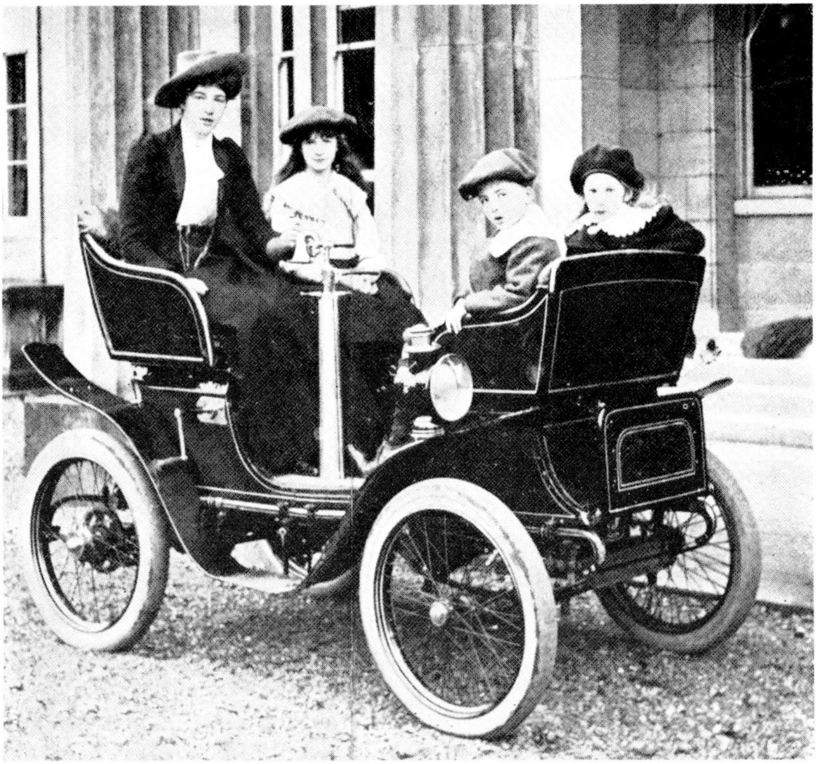

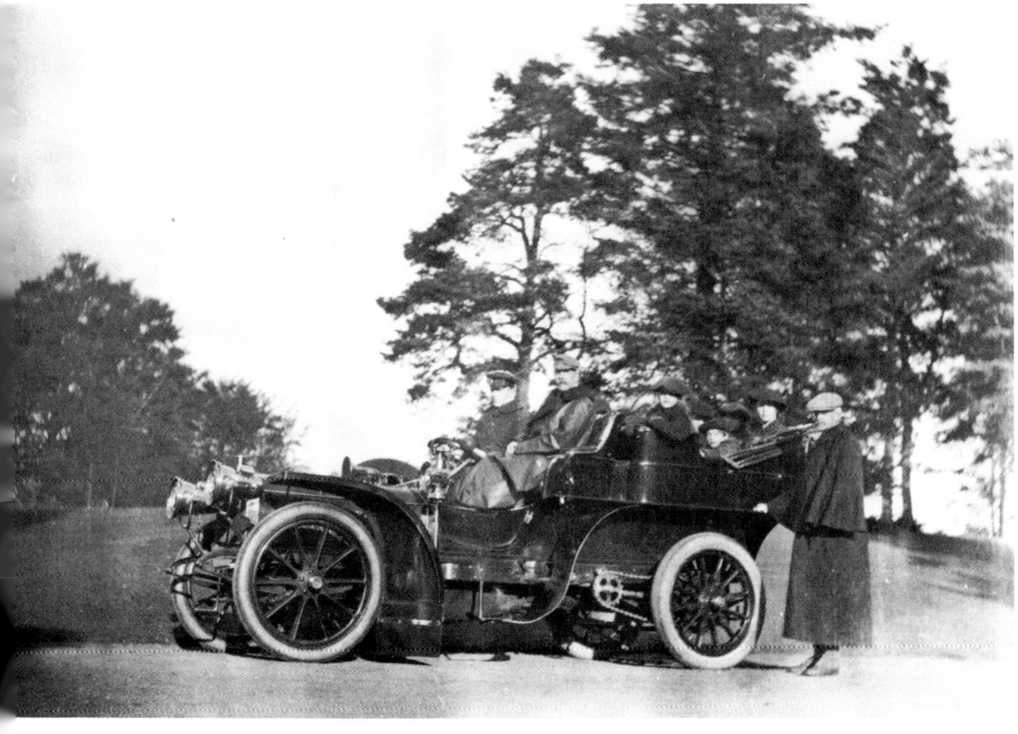

JOHN BULL. "H'M! PRETTY STATE OF THINGS THIS! ONE CREW

—APRIL 1, 1903.

TO PIECES, AND THE OTHER NOT IN SIGHT!"

49 A J Balfour, as Prime Minister, pictured by *Punch* in one sporting activity in which he did not participate!

50 A J Balfour starting for a motor ride.

"I am uneasy about my affairs"

Balfour became Prime Minister upon the retirement of his uncle, Lord Salisbury, in July 1902 and remained in that office until the autumn of 1905. The ensuing election resulted in a crushing defeat for the Conservatives. His Premiership, in many ways, was the least glorious part of his political career. As Winston Churchill put it, he had succeeded to "an exhausted inheritance" and he was neither particularly interested in nor able to take the lead in the Tariff Reform controversy which was splitting his party. The distant and urbane nature of the man did not allow for undue concern. Ramsay MacDonald made the telling comment upon Balfour's death, "He saw a great deal of life from afar."

There is no evidence that political defeat distressed him unduly. He had his wide ranging interests and much to do at Whittingehame. It is not until shortly before the First World War that cracks start to appear in the fabric of family life of there. In 1909, A J wrote from Biarritz to his sister-in-law, Lady Betty, following a letter from her about "the difficulties and frictions which sometimes mar the harmony of our family life." There was clearly dissatisfaction within the ranks of the younger members of the household. A J suggests inviting some young men to join the company at Whittingehame and his observations seem to hark directly back to his own youth and The Souls, "It can't be right to give the young things no society but that of their parents, an uncle of sixty and an occasional M P. I really don't see what is the use of a big country house, with five new baths and a lift, unless you employ it as a meeting ground between youths and maidens. However, have it your own way - *I* am not their mother."[37]

The approach of war and social change were keenly felt in such a politically aware house. The year 1914 shows early signs of turbulence. Oswald has just joined the 60th Rifles at Aldershot after passing out from Sandhurst a few weeks before the outbreak of war and, on March 6, his mother, Lady Frances, writes: "I can hardly write of the other event of the week. It has made me both ill and unhappy. The *complete* destruction of Whitekirk by the suffragettes. It has roused the deepest feeling that has yet been felt. Betty and I are going in for a fund for its restoration by suffragists . . .". The ancient church was burned down in the early hours of February 26: the minister found a hammer and a knife at the back of the church together with a note bearing the message, "By torturing the finest and noblest women in the country you are driving more women into rebellion." Frances felt deep pain at the destruction of the nearby, ancient church, the joy of 19 generations of worshippers over its 570 years of existence - especially in terms of her own and her sister-in-law's general commitment to the cause in which it was destroyed. She and Betty must have been hurt to the quick by the Reverend Rankin's observation: "What the hand of no Scotsman has ever attempted, the hands of Scotswomen have succeeded in doing."[38]

The outbreak of war brings much trepidation and excitement to Whittingehame. The household staff at Carlton Gardens are evacuated to Whittingehame against a background of fears of invasion. On August 20 1914, in a letter headed 'The 15th Day of War', Betty writes: "Yesterday at lunch we were called by Baker, the butler, to see a hospital ship steaming down the Forth. The maids in the double attic said they heard firing between 2 and 3 . . . ." Then the telephone had rung with news from (East) Linton that "something was going on in the Forth". At this news the family set off in the Napier to investigate the situation. On the shore at Tyninghame they were a trifle disappointed to find nought but two sleeping sentries, although there were groups of territorials on the road and in the villages. All the talk was of invasion. At East Linton, Betty visits the local doctor and learns that "the territorials are quartered in the drill hall, the school and the Church Hall. They lie at night on the bare floor . . . ." She is alarmed to learn that they must sleep in their clothes, have no bedlinen and no washing facilities save those in the river. And, she notes disapprovingly, "They visit the public house too much." It is agreed that books and magazines will be sent down to the village from the House so that the soldiery might improve their minds.

Good works in the cause of the War become a new and important feature of life. The double attic at the top of the servants' stair is made over for the use of working parties. "The work party was assembled in the double attic between 7.30 and 9.30. About 16 women were stitching shirts and making socks. Aunt Alice wound wool. Mary, my daughter, Joan, my niece, and Nell, my second daughter, were perched on a table, sewing too. I read war news from the newspaper," reports Lady Betty in her correspondence.

In September there comes the news that Oswald Balfour has been wounded in action and the minister, Dr Robertson, visits the working party to offer prayers. His visit was not entirely welcome. "He said his prayer would be very short, and it was eternally long. Most of us standing up, with shirts and stockings in our hands."[39]

The high spot of the day is the arrival of *The Scotsman* in the morning. Blanche Dugdale says, "The Daily Paper comes into the dining room - we linger over breakfast until it *does* come." The arrival of the two copies of *The Scotsman* appears to provoke a daily battle with the adults first in the pecking order. "The delay of getting news of the casualties was more than the two girls could stand so they have now taken in a 3rd paper between them. Joy on their faces when Baker handed it to them this morning." Some mornings, when a particular piece of news is expected, then even the adult members of the household are unable to contain themselves and they telephone down to Dr Wedderburn in East Linton for the news from *The Scotsman*, one hour ahead of the Whittingehame delivery.

There is great anticipation when the telegraph brings news of an impending visit by one of Joan's cousins, Captain Leveson Gower, whose torpedo destroyer is laid up and under repair at Leith. To the curiosity of the well groomed children, he sports four weeks' beard, and one observes that he "would certainly be taken for a Russian", who are rumoured to have landed. Indeed, Leveson Gower confirms that he has heard that the Russians have landed at Aberdeen and are moving "through the Island" to join battle on the Western Front.

Fears of invasion are everywhere. A former servant at the House, Wharton, writes to Alice Balfour from Scarborough of the attack by the German navy on the town in December 1914 - "hundreds of people have left Scarborough" - and sends a piece of shell from a crater near her house.[40]

Even in the early days of War, the toll it is to take becomes apparent. On September 2, Lady Frances writes to her son Frank: "Every day one takes more and more God given comfort that if we are to lose our men it is in a great and spirited cause . . . Whitt. is wonderful in always being the same, but as all changes, and the ranks thin, and the young go forth, there is something stifling in Alice . . . ." Whittingehame may represent continuity in turbulent times but the same personal differences are in evidence.[39]

Family life at Whittingehame survives those early days of the War. By the end of August 1914, two of A J's nephews are on active service: Oswald in France with the Expeditionary Force and Arthur Strutt, second son of Lord and Lady Rayleigh, is at sea. December 1914 sees the last family Christmas of the War at Whittingehame. The wounded Oswald returns home from the front and before the end of the holiday the nephews and nieces accompany their uncle on a trip to a battle cruiser squadron lying in the Firth of Forth where they were all guests of Admiral Sir David Beatty, taking lunch afterwards on Lady Beatty's yacht anchored off Rosyth. From now on, the War was to leave the House comparatively quiet and the life within its walls was never to be quite the same.

Also, financial difficulties now manifest themselves. James Balfour's original fortune, which had grown to something like £3 million when A J Balfour inherited, had been largely dissipated by unwise investments and the increasing cost of running the sizeable establishments at Whittingehame and Carlton Gardens. As early as 1895, Alice had brought A J B to task over finances. Looking through the accounts she saw that the outgoings on the house and estate exceeded the income generated by the estate by £2,000 for both 1894 and 1895, and told Arthur "it could not last".[41] In the last two decades of his life, Balfour became increasingly worried by his deteriorating financial position. There is much correspondence from both A J and Eustace evincing worries about their finances before the First War. In 1913, he confided in Lady Elcho, "I am uneasy about my affairs," and in July of that year he wrote to Alice of his fears for the future of private estates in East Lothian. "I greatly fear that when Lord Wemyss dies Gosford will follow Yester: and that (if peat fails), Whittingehame will follow Gosford. May it be otherwise ordained !"

For many years he and his brother Gerald took an almost obsessive interest in business plans to dry and thus convert peat into a commercial fuel and more than £250,000 was lost in two unsuccessful ventures, Wet Carbonising and Peco. Before the outbreak of the War, Wet Carbonising was in difficulties and in the 1920s tho other venture, Peco, also failed. The connection of the Balfours with Wet Carbonising brought some criticism of them in the press during 1917. *Truth* magazine pointed out that following the company's signature of a contract with the War Office the previously unquoted shares of one shilling each had shot to 70 shillings on the Stock Market. But, with equal rapidity, they were to subside again to one shilling.

51 The village of Whittingehame in the snow, 1902.

Speculation and gambling held a strange excitement for the otherwise prudent Balfour. He used to visit the Casino at Cannes and invested in many dubious companies on the London and New York Stock Exchanges: his own personal account books contain lists of courageous investments in South and Central American railroads, African mining concerns and companies exploiting new and untried technology. When Lord Beaverbrook went to see him on political business in 1911, the newspaper magnate complained afterwards, "He would talk of nothing but the stock markets, with special reference to to the chances of making a big killing on the New York Stock Exchange." In August 1914, Balfour writes from Carlton Gardens, "I am rather embarrassed about Barings (the London bankers) and the £10,000 . . . but it is, of course, a flea bite . . . there was not an institution in London - from the Bank of England downwards, which was not in peril of closing its doors on Saturday."[37]

Gerald Balfour does not take the situation so philosophically. He wrote to his wife, Betty, on August 13 from Cadoxton in south Wales: "I have arranged to see Arthur Tuesday for discussion of finance . . . the position is very difficult and seems desperate to me, but I will not give up hope."[39]

By the end of the First War, although the situation

has been contained it is, in fact, becoming even more serious and long term in scale. There is a general decline in what the family can afford. Alice has clearly fired a broadside about the costs of running the house: the House account is overdrawn and she wishes to know what is to be done. A J writes from Paris in June 1919: "The last thing I want to do is have big, formal parties, but I should be sorry if the family could not come when they wanted, and odds and ends of people are always turning up . . . as to the money side of the question, it is impossible to say where I stand." On top of all this, it is impossible to buy coal because of the rationing applying to big houses and, as Balfour readily admits, "the fireplaces at Whittingehame are very extravagant". He suggests that Alice should put stoves into the larger rooms: which would burn a range of solid fuels and which course of action he advises their friend Lady Beatty has already undertaken.[42]

In his declining years, Balfour found his investments falling in value; rents ceasing to be productive; and the cost of running Carlton Gardens and Whittingehame an increasing drain on finances. For the first time, he was becoming concerned over the future of Whittingehame House. Although there were adequate funds to exist, the great fortune he had inherited was now exhausted and a great question mark hung over House and estate. Nevertheless, he was still, as ever, dreaming of improvements. In 1919, he is instructing Alice "to overhaul the tennis court" and to get a price for turning the asphalt court into a "normal hard court" on which he thinks guests would much rather play. The urge to continue spending seems quite undiminished by the actual financial situation.

Despite financial difficulties, he would still take a generous view when something arose which others might have viewed less scrupulously. Until very recently, Traprain Law, an impressive and ancient rocky outcrop standing some 350 feet high, was on the estate and it was with A J Balfour's support and encouragement that excavations were undertaken which were to reveal not only the fact that it had been a fortified home in prehistoric days, but also the famed Traprain treasure of beautiful silver vessels. The Society of Antiquaries of Scotland began the excavation in 1914 and over two summers stone, bronze and iron relics were found, suggesting that the site was occupied as long ago as the late Stone Age. Roman coins bearing the head of the Emperor Arcadius (395-408) were found but there was no evidence of actual Roman occupation, which suggests they were stolen. The First War necessitated the breaking off of excavations, which were

52 The arts and crafts movement, patronised so enthusiastically by Arthur and Eustace Balfour from its earliest days, was the butt of much satirical comment, as in this *Punch* cartoon.

resumed in 1919. After only a couple of weeks the remarkable discovery was made. A foreman who was loosening some foundation work located a piece of metal and up came a silver bowl. A pit some two feet in diameter and one and a half feet deep was then uncovered and there was found silver dishes, bowls, flagons and chalices. Much of the hoard, which appeared to have been hurriedly concealed, had been flattened and the evidence of the 160 pieces of silver suggested that it was all the fruits of plunder. Again some coins indicated that the deposit was made some time around the beginning of the fifth century. This was a unique find discovered as a result of Balfour's interest and encouragement and he was delighted to hear of the discovery. He wrote to Alice from France in 1919 greatly interested by her news of the finds and advised that he had written to Strathearn, his solicitor, to find out the situation as regards "Scotch treasure trove". Whatever the position, there was no question of claiming treasure trove and he was resolved that the treasure should be deposited at the National Museum of Antiquities in Edinburgh (where it is on display to this day).

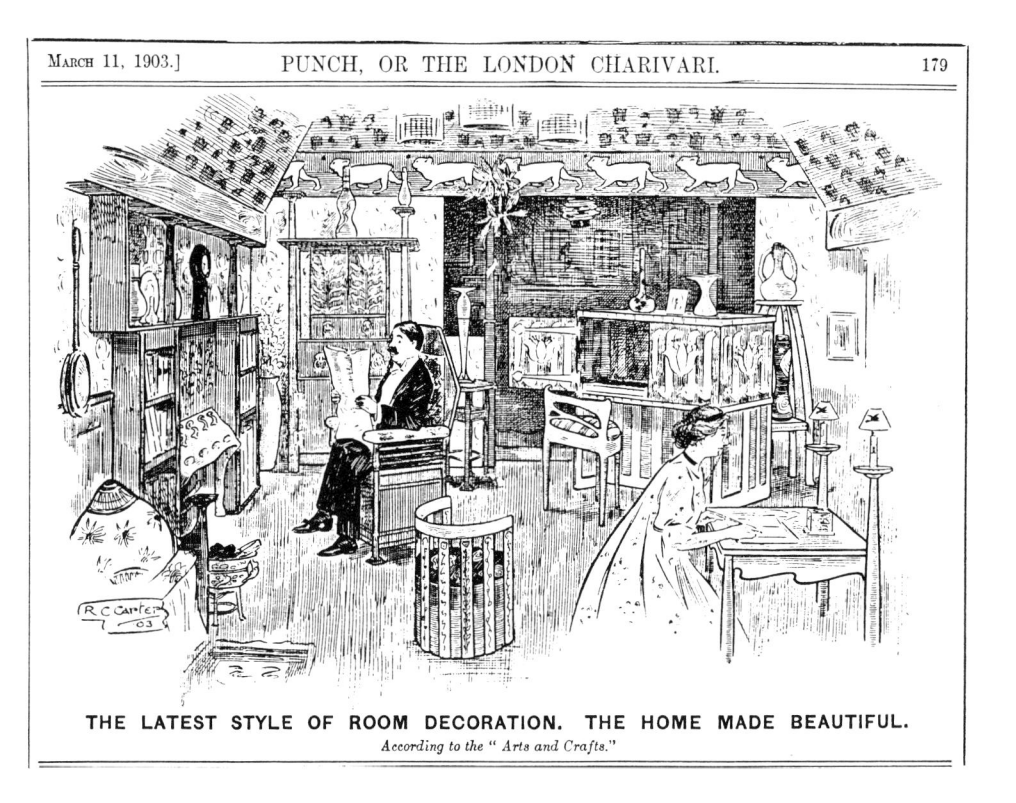

MARCH 11, 1903.]   PUNCH, OR THE LONDON CHARIVARI.   179

THE LATEST STYLE OF ROOM DECORATION. THE HOME MADE BEAUTIFUL.
According to the " Arts and Crafts."

A political decision which was, quite literally, to shake the world was formulated at Whittingehame towards the end of the War. In August 1917, the Balfour Declaration, committing the British Government irrevocably to the establishment of a Jewish homeland in Palestine, was drafted in the study on the ground floor (not, in fact, by Leopold Amery who rather fraudulently claimed the credit for the document when it was accepted by the Cabinet in November).

On May 5 1922, A J Balfour was raised to the peerage as Earl of Balfour and Viscount Traprain of Whittingehame, "with remainder in default of issue male to his brother the Right Hon. Gerald William Balfour and heirs male of his body." In November 1922 the tenantry of the Estate met in the library of the House and presented an illuminated address to commemorate the elevation to the peerage and his services at the Washington Conference.

Life at the House continues despite the absence of youth and gaiety. In October 1924, Lady Frances is told by a surgeon in Edinburgh that she is suffering from breast cancer and the next month she courageously submits to the operation. The same month, W Hedley Smith, the factor at Whittingehame dies. And Alice is becoming progressively more deaf. Despite all these reverses, Frances notes in her correspondence whilst recovering that "Whitt. Life is the same. The Woods decay, glorious in death, the air is still and peace is in the air." [43] Arthur asks his nephew "Ral" to take over as factor from Hedley Smith, and this appointment, together with the latter's progress in accountancy in Edinburgh, means that he is able to become engaged that year to Jean Cooke Yarborough.

It would be misleading to suggest that life had become boring and depressing at Whittingehame. Drama and excitement still intruded. In December 1924, Lady Betty's leg was broken in two places when she was felled by an apple tree in the orchard which was, in its turn, being felled by the young son of a house guest. She was carried back to the House on an improvised stretcher and her leg set, under chloroform, in her bedroom, to which she was confined for many weeks.[43]

Other house guests in 1924 occasioned great excitement. In August, a friend of the family from East Anglia, Mrs O Kahn, was staying with her friend, a certain Mrs Joshua. Mr Joshua had been left in London and did not accompany his spouse. A telephone call came to Whittingehame and Mrs Kahn went to the telephone box to learn that Mr Joshua had been found shot dead, together

53 The Balfour Declaration, drafted at Whittingehame, August 1917.

Foreign Office,
November 2nd, 1917.

Dear Lord Rothschild,

I have much pleasure in conveying to you, on behalf of His Majesty's Government, the following declaration of sympathy with Jewish Zionist aspirations which has been submitted to, and approved by, the Cabinet.

"His Majesty's Government view with favour the establishment in Palestine of a national home for the Jewish people, and will use their best endeavours to facilitate the achievement of this object, it being clearly understood that nothing shall be done which may prejudice the civil and religious rights of existing non-Jewish communities in Palestine, or the rights and political status enjoyed by Jews in any other country".

I should be grateful if you would bring this declaration to the knowledge of the Zionist Federation.

[signature: Arthur James Balfour]

with his servant at the servant's flat, and with an unsigned cheque in the hand of the former. Mrs Kahn lacked the courage to tell her friend of the circumstances of her husband's demise and returned to the dining room to say that her husband had been killed in a motor accident. Alas, the newly bereaved Mrs Joshua, returning home by train, bought a newspaper at the station in Carlisle and was apprised of the shocking and mysterious circumstances.[44]

Another visitor in the late 1920s is A J's old friend Winston S Churchill who stayed at the House and painted in the area. There were two paintings of Balfour started at Whittingehame and finished in Churchill's studio, an oil of the Forth and some sketches, all of which owed their inspiration and execution to his visits. Churchill referred to these later visits in *Great Contemporaries*: "I had the privilege of visiting him several times during the last months of his life. I saw with grief the approaching departure, and - for all human purposes - extinction of a being high-uplifted above the common run."

The fabric of country house life was visibly wearing. In this, of course, Balfour was not alone. Hundreds of families in Britain looked upon a similar uncertain future after the First World War: not only the finances but the very way of the world was changing before their eyes. But for the newly created Earl, health and financial worries crowded in together and became entwined. He complained about the quality of life at the House in his last year, the "Cripples' Home" as he called it where all the guests seemed to be "blind, deaf, halt or maim." Lady Frances Balfour, although still as perspicacious as ever, was also now elderly and enjoying even more indifferent health than before, as was Eve Balfour. In October 1928, Blanche writes of the visit of Lord Dawson from Harley Street, in the company of the local doctor from East Linton, Dr Wedderburn. Dawson impressed her. "You also feel the *experience* of a man who is accustomed to dealing with patients of the Nunky type - patients whose intellects are so much part of them that it is no good catering for the body and ignoring the mind." To the delight of all the household apart from Alice, Dawson prescribes claret at meals and champagne, albeit the latter only every three days. The cellar keys are to be handed over to Ral and Blanche notes that this will save "an infinity of friction and bother".[45]

There were, however, still a few bright spots. In February 1928 a contract was signed with Cassells, the London publishers, to write a major two-volume autobiography. Balfour optimistically observed, "I shall now expect the money to come flowing in." In fact, the projected two volume work was never to be finished, although one rather slim volume was to be completed by Blanche Dugdale and published posthumously.

September of 1928 saw the last autumn family gathering at Whittingehame. Lady Frances writes of being collected at East Linton station by Mills in the new Rolls Royce and although she found Arthur hoarse with his worsening throat trouble, "his companionship was as stimulating, as amusing and as loveable as ever." He was restricted to his room some of the time, the family taking it in turns to amuse him, but when he was able there were long drives in the surrounding countryside in the Rolls. As well as the Rolls, he had received a new gramaphone from the family - "never was £35 better spent" - and Lady Frances wrote that both gifts brought "many hours of real happiness to the last 2 years of AJB's life." A J regularly despatched members of the family and guests into Edinburgh to buy new records. One day, Beethoven's Fifth Symphony appeared at the House. He sat and listened all the way through and then declared, "I certainly get *as much* pleasure from that performance as the real thing."[44]

House guests were now much fewer although that September brought one of the last - and some light relief. Frances records "a series of idiotic telegrams from the tennis player Mlle. Alvarez," apparently about to arrive in the neighbourhood and announcing her intention to visit at some unspecified day and hour. Uninvited guests were as unwelcome as ever. "I privately wish Mlle. Alvarez was at the bottom of the sea." One house guest, Ian Malcolm, who had written a short political appreciation of Lord Balfour, had only just left when the crunching of gravel at the front door announced another visitor. From a chauffeur-driven Rolls Royce, laden with trunks and suitcases, elegantly stepped the world's number three tennis player. Once inside the House, she apprised the occupants of the fact that she had driven 280 miles "to see dear Lord Balfour for two minutes" ! Blanche takes up the story. The senorita, "a very good looking woman - about 24, beautiful clothes, beautiful figure", accepted tea "eagerly" and was then admitted to A J B in his study. There she equally eagerly announced she had nowhere to stay that night and was, of course, hospitably invited to stay, although not without misgivings on the part of the head of the household - sister Alice being away and unaware of developments. And there was also the matter of a maid and a chauffeur to be accommodated.

"The Senorita began to tell us how characteristic and charming was the *hospitality* of English (sic.) country houses. 'No fuss, no bother, you make guests so welcome'." At this point more crunching on gravel heralded the arrival of Alice. "Who is this? Anuzza guest ?" quizzes the Senorita. Alice's reaction in the hall outside is predictable. "*Hang* the woman ! What insolence !" Over dinner, however, the Senorita proceeds to salvage the jaundiced view taken of her. She turns out to be a brilliant conversationalist - if a little exhausting - and a self-professed expert on virtually every subject touched upon. She even professes to be a philosopher and to be writing a book on

54 First notes by Balfour for for his autobiography, made at Whittingehame, 1928.

the subject, which she proposes to send to the author of *The Foundations of Belief* and *A Defence of Philosophic Doubt* ! She steers the conversation around the dinner table from books and pictures to people and places. She talks of her expertise at tennis, skating, swimming and billiards. Those at Whittingehame have never met anybody quite like this enthusiastic, archetypal twenties girl "absolutely naive, afraid of nothing and nobody ... serenely certain she is a success in every direction."[44]

There was still the capacity to be amused in the most adverse of circumstances. At the end of August 1928, A J returned from an X-ray and a particularly painful throat examination in Edinburgh to find one of the Whittingehame fire drills in progress. One housemaid descended the fire escape over energetically and landed heavily on the lawn, breaking her false teeth, much to everyone's amusement.

Another source of pleasure to A J was his young great-nephew Gerald (later to be 4th Earl of Balfour). Lady Frances recorded in October 1928 that "little Gerald was here for tea, showed Nunky picture books and explained them, Nunky able to understand a great many of his words, and highly pleased by doing so."

Some days now he was alive and totally aware of the world around him. Other days he was old and hoarse and feeble. The era of sparkle had come to an end.

55 The Earl of Balfour with his great-nephew Gerald (4th Earl) on the terrace at Whittingehame, 1928.

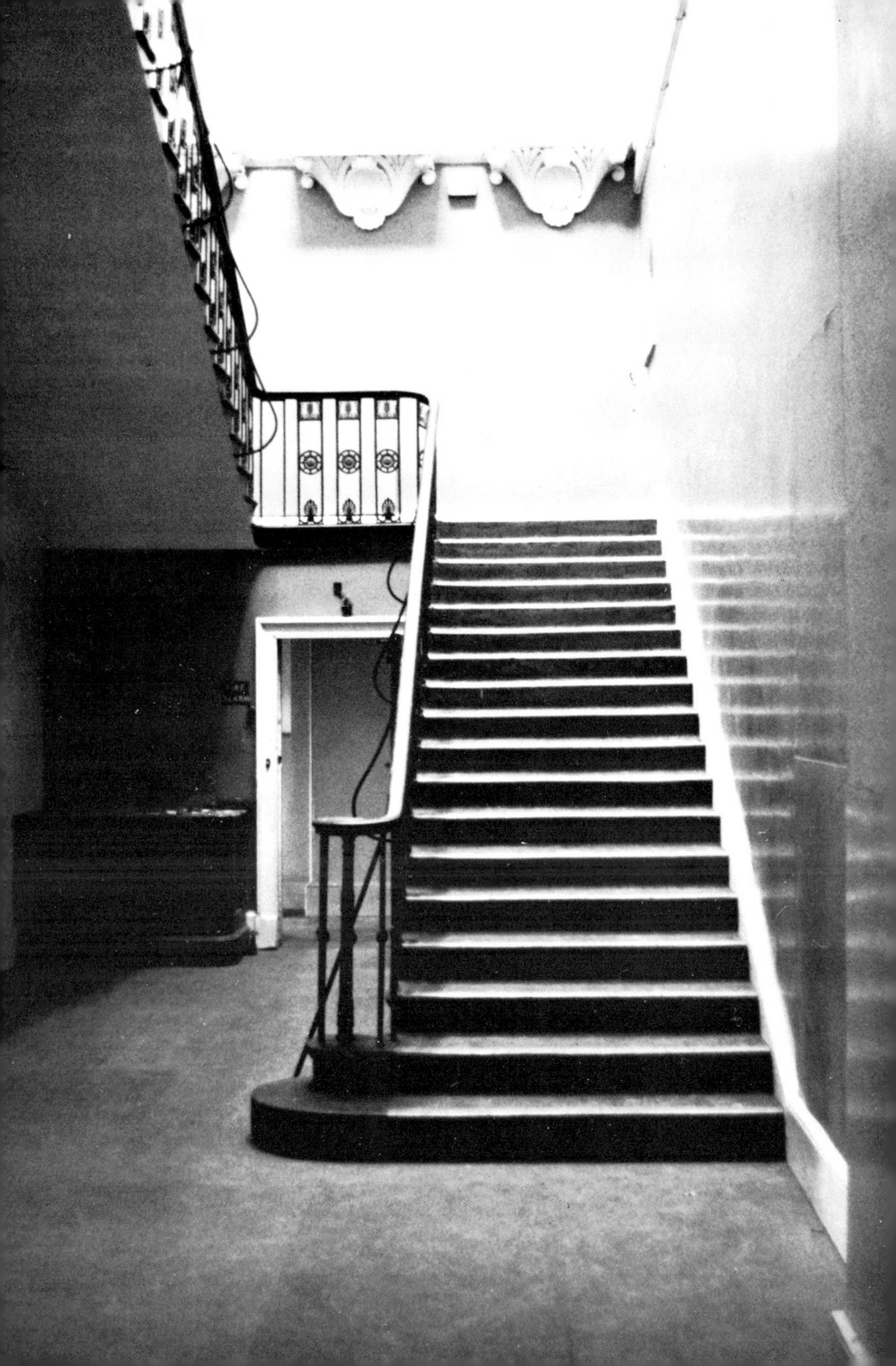

"Less adaptable . . ."

The first Earl of Balfour died in London on March 19 1930. The last visitors included Chaim Weizmann, whose cause for the Jewish homeland Balfour had identified himself with so closely, and his personal servant James Coleman. He asked Coleman to look after his beloved Whittingehame to the best of his ability. Westminster Abbey was offered for burial but it was Arthur Balfour's wish that his body be brought back to Whittingehame for interment in the family's private burial ground, within the grounds of the House where his mother, Lady Blanche, and his brothers Frank and Eustace were buried. There was a service at Whittingehame Church and then the body was hauled across the covering of spring snow on a cart drawn by two Clydesdale horses.

Balfour's political career had been distinguished by any benchmark. He had held cabinet rank for 27 years: longer than Winston Churchill, Gladstone, Lord Palmerston, Lord Liverpool or the younger Pitt. Apart from the highest political office in the land, he had also variously served as Secretary for Scotland, Chief Secretary for Ireland, Foreign Secretary, First Lord of the Admiralty, First Lord of the Treasury and Leader of the House. His practised languour and the relative ease with which he was able to approach intellectual problems, often misled his critics into regarding him as idle and unambitious, mistakenly cast in the old English mould of landed gentry turned politicos. But this view ignored that sharpness of intellect, skill in debate and political courage all of which contributed to successes in Ireland, with the Education Act of 1902 and in the adoption of the Balfour Declaration. It is, perhaps, these three single achievements which stand out as the highlights of a packed political career.

As provided for, his brother Gerald became the second Earl and nephew Ral and his family moved back to the House from Redcliff in the hope of keeping the establishment going. It had, of course, been one of Balfour's last wishes that the family might remain living in the House he had loved so much. On February 25 1931, Lady Frances Balfour died and was buried at Whittingehame near to her brother-in-law. The sale of individual items of

56 The main staircase after the House was vacated.

furniture, books and china began in an effort to make ends meet. In April 1932, the family journal records sadly that a favourite painting by Edward Burne-Jones entitled *The Wheel of Fortune* has been sold. The large oil, 78 x 39 in., started by Burne-Jones in 1875, first exhibited at the Grosvenor Gallery in 1883, and which was one of the few Burne Jones pictures to be hung at Whittingehame, as opposed to Carlton Gardens, was sold for £1,200.[46]

A ten year period was agreed with the Inland Revenue for the payment of death duties but, even still, there was insufficient cash to keep the House going. In 1935, Ral decided that the large House would have to be vacated and the family moved back to Redcliff where he and his family had lived prior to his uncle's death. A J Balfour's personal servant, Coleman, was put in charge of the House and he and his family went to live in the basement, now the sole occupiers of the building. There was great sadness in the family. According to the family journal for that year written by Blanche, "Auntie Jean felt that the house was asking to be lived in and enjoyed", but this was not to be. At one point, Ral returned from London in a state of great depression with plans to sell the House in a bid to meet the family debts. In fact, the family did manage to hold onto the House but its days as a great country house were over. And in 1936 Alice, who had so meticulously run the House for so many years, died and was interred in the family burial ground.

In 1938, a three day sale by auction of the furniture and some of the fittings of the House was announced by Dowells, the Edinburgh auctioneers. In the event, the September Munich crisis forced the postponement of the sale and it did not go ahead until October 4. And so, the House was was stripped of its fine furnishings, either sold or removed to Redcliff.

Whittingehame House was now made available to a project to create a farm training centre for Jewish refugee children who might thus be prepared for further emigration overseas - primarily to Palestine. House and grounds, together with sufficient farm land for a home farm were leased on generous terms and Lord Balfour made training facilities available elsewhere on the estate. The Whittingehame Farm School, financed by Scottish Jews and operated by the Whittingehame Farm School Ltd under the chairmanship of Captain Robert Solomon, was opened at the beginning of 1939 with an initial intake of just 51 children. This number quickly increased to 96, including 31 girls, as youngsters between the ages of 14 and 17, fleeing Nazi persecution in Germany and Czechoslovakia, were assigned places. Between three and four hundred passed through the House between January 1939 and September 1941, with a normal establishment of some 160. Lord and Lady Balfour identified themselves closely with the project and ensured that there was a warm welcome for the refugees. "They were of all types of colouring, dark or fair, freckled or sallow; tubby or slender; some typically Jewish, some golden- haired and Nordic-featured; none could speak a word of English, so we had to rely on smiles and friendly hand-shaking at frequent intervals. But every one of them had his hidden personal tragedy in the background, each was profoundly alone," wrote Lady Balfour.

By the end of the summer of 1939 blackout material was pinned to the back of all the shutters in the House as Whittingehame prepared again for war. The happy life of the farm school is reflected in a 50th anniversary booklet which tells of the farming, the dairy work and the vegetable growing. For recreation there was football, table tennis and chess. During that first summer Lady Balfour had her forester fell some trees at the Whittingehame Water and dam the river to make an open-air swimming pool. In the winter there was sledging and, in some secrecy, skating on the ice.[47]

Even in such a remote community there were some savage reminders of war. After the Germans had overrun the Low Countries in May 1940 many of the staff and older boys at Whittingehame were deemed to be "enemy aliens", notwithstanding the fact that they had been forced to flee Nazi Germany, and 36 of them were taken from the House under armed guard and transported to Lingfield Race Course where they were interned alongside German seamen, many of them hardcore Nazis. The Home Secretary revoked the order in the middle of August and they were allowed to return to Whittingehame "stronger in our beliefs".

Many nights the German bombers came over off the North Sea on their way to bomb the industrial west of Scotland and, one night, a returning bomber dropped its cargo at the nearby farm of Papple. In September 1939, the first enemy aircraft to be shot down over Britain was brought down in the Lammermuir Hills not far away following an unsuccessful attack on the Forth bridge. On such occasions the entire school would retreat down the stairs to the basement of the House. There was constant vigilance and everyone took their turn at ARP work. "Having to do the night rounds and walking round the house when all was still and the rest of the people were sleeping. Then we who were on duty would go outside as well to hear if there was anything going on in the sky.

The most beautiful time of all was a clear winter's night with the moon and stars so bright that one could almost read a newspaper. So cold and clear with snow underfoot and we never felt the cold."[47]

One of these children at the Farm School was called Harry Nomburg, who was born in Coburg in central Germany and who had lived in Berlin. He had escaped from Germany in 1939 and came to Whittingehame to work at the farm school. He was later recruited to a top secret unit known as X-Troop at the age of 19 and was parachuted back behind German lines.[48] Many of the children were to succeed in settling in Palestine after the war and in a very real sense they represented the wartime spearhead of the Zionist movement. "Whittingehame I consider the happiest year of my life in retrospect: the cameraderie, simplicity, and last unaffected and carefree year of my youth, the Chaluzik spirit with its enthusiasm, singing religious services, dancing and emerging puberty," wrote one attendee fifty years later. And some of the boys and girls at the school found their partners for life at Whittingehame . . .[47]

In late 1942 Dr Guthrie's Institution for Boys moved into the building after extensive roof repairs and general maintenance carried out by George Rae & Co. of Edinburgh under the instruction of the Ministry of Works.[49] Dr Guthrie's was to remain until 1953: as a result there were a number of interesting and later infamous residents, including the notorious professional criminal in the making, Walter Scott Ellis, and his brother William Shakespeare Ellis. Despite their literary nomenclature, efforts in the outside world were directed into other areas. In 1966, Walter Scott Ellis, at the age of 34, with a record of 19 previous convictions and many acquittals behind him, was sentenced by Lord Hunter to twenty-one years in prison for organised and armed bank robbery. At the time this was the longest sentence handed down in Scotland. And in November 1950 there was the particularly nasty and gruesome death of one of the young dining room maids, murdered and horribly mutilated by a jealous under-chef.

Until 1948, the main approach to the House was from the north at the side of and following the line of the lime tree avenue: the present entrance was a service one only. In the floods of 1947-8 Gilpin's original wooden bridge connecting the main drive was undermined and washed away.

After 1953 the house lay empty again until a new batch of refugees arrived - this time from the 1956 Hungarian revolution - and the aroma of *bortsch* soup hung heavy in the long halls and passages. But they were soon empty again: until 1963 when the Balfour family finally decided to sell the property and some 45 acres surrounding it.

The purchaser, for the sum of £11,500, was Holt School for Boys, which moved from Jardine Hall near Lockerbie in the Easter Holiday of 1964 "with 95 boys, several pantechnicons and much enthusiasm". The building was, of course, well suited to its role as a boys' school with its central passages, large rooms for dormitories and classrooms and extensive grounds. Until the Summer Term of 1980 the house became 'home' to a numerically variable complement of boys - at its lowest point in December 1969 there were only 65 and in 1979 there were 145. Some were sons of expatriates abroad, others the sons of NCOs in the Services. As the Headmaster observed, "Some had been at eight or nine schools before they came to us at age eleven." Many were from from warmer climes abroad and the cold passages and the rows of showers and washbasins in the basement of the House

57 Holt School Young Farmers' Club. Even the sheep wore ties!

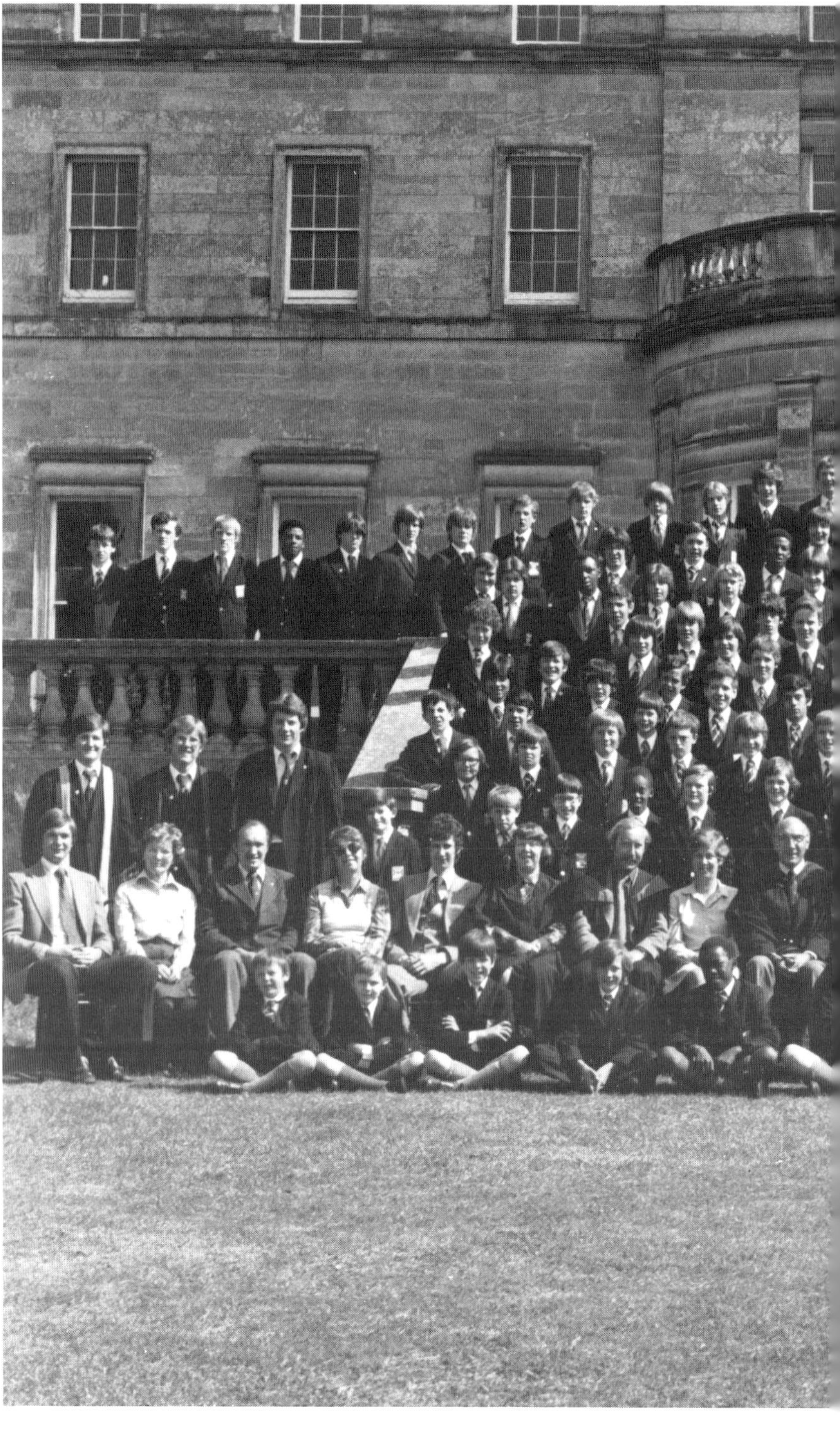

115

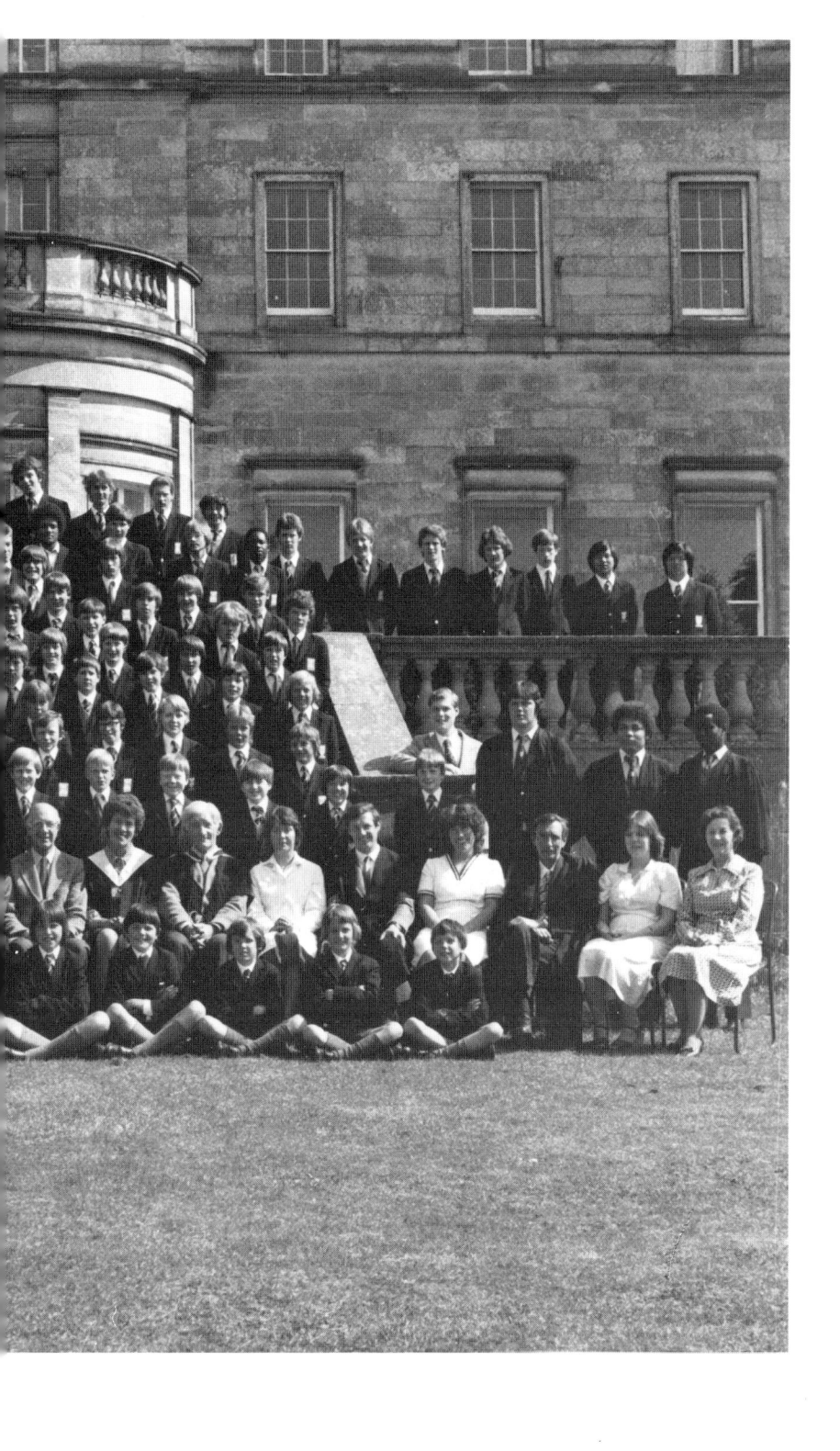

must have seemed a harsh regime to bear ! There were boys from Zambia, Nigeria, Malawi, Kenya and Uganda, as well as a number of Asian birth. On one occasion, the Education Attache from the Zambian High Commission in London referred to Holt School as "a United Nations in miniature". The presence of the African boys played a major part in the School's athletic success. In 1972, a Junior Department for eight to ten year-olds was opened.

The Headmasters, Mr Witherow until 1969 and Lawrence Read thereafter, would appear to have tried their level best to maintain standards, as the latter put it in the school magazine in 1974: "To give in to the demands of modern youth is not always to that youth's advantage in the long run, and while I am prepared to listen and, where thought reasonable, accede to the requests of the school, I am not prepared to forego the best, to my mind at least, aspects and traditions of boarding school life." It is fortunate that sixteen years of boarding school life did not take a heavier toll of Whittingehame House. Indeed, according to a reading of the school magazine, it brought new and occasionally dramatic life into the building with bonfires, fireworks, the Leslie brothers returning from Zambia with "rabies (suspected) contracted after biting their dog", Sports Days, Bacon attempting "to emulate the birds", whatever that was, and performances of *The Importance of Being Earnest*.[50] There was strong support for the School's archery, fencing and Young Farmers' Clubs. In 1980, the Headmaster and owner, Lawrence Read, decided to close the school in the face of economic recession and the prospect of a falling roll. The House became empty again when the last coach went down the drive in June 1980. Lawrence Read reflects on Whittingehame, "I truly believe that as a school it saw its finest hours, for it provided a beautiful home and fine grounds for hundreds of boys."

At the end of 1981, it was purchased, together with some of the land and associated buildings, for £90,230 by an Arab sheikh, Mohammed al-Abdaly, and in 1982, a £7 million plan to turn it into a 75-bed private hospital for rich Arabs was announced. The Sheikh, who was known by locals at Stenton's Oak Inn as 'Lawrence of Arabia in the snow', after the style of his customary nocturnal return to Whittingehame in full Arab dress after several pints of lager, was particularly tickled at the prospect of caring for his fellow Arabs in the same house as the Balfour Declaration had originated. The plans included new buildings, a helicopter landing pad, limousine parking, gymnasium, sauna and solarium and tennis courts with tunnels to connect the facilities.

58 *Previous page*: Holt School for Boys. The last year, 1979-80, photographed on the south terrace.

According to *The Glasgow Herald*, "The whisky drinking sheikh wanted to import Saudi tile-layers, Japanese electricians and Korean trench diggers to play a part in its preparation as a luxury hospital." [51] The plan was said to be backed by the German Krupps armament business fortune but, on January 26 1982, East Lothian District Council in Haddington issued a notice of refusal of planning permission on the grounds that the development would have a detrimental effect upon the local Health Services and resources, particularly upon the availability of qualified and experienced nursing staff in the Lothian Health Board area. The backers pulled out. The company involved, Thamoud Ltd., went into receivership the same week as the Secretary of State for Scotland reversed the local planners' decision. The Secretary of State for Scotland, Mr George Younger, after an inquiry into the matter, took the view that the reason for the refusal of the application was not a planning matter and was therefore invalid. "The Secretary of State regards the main planning issues as relating to the proposed use of a virtually unoccupied Category A Listed Building . . . and he can see no reason why planning permission for this purpose was refused."[52] A blatantly political decision had been taken under the cloak of planning law. Although the Secretary of State used his powers to grant planning permission over the heads of the politicians of East Lothian District Council, the news came too late and the future of the House was put into jeopardy. A liquidator was appointed in June 1983 by the Court of Session upon the application of the Bank of Scotland which was owed £109,000, and a firm of Edinburgh architects who had been working on the project for the Sheikh, G R M Kennedy & Partners, also took action for £36,000 in unpaid fees. Appropriately enough, Thamoud is referred to, in The Koran, as an ancient Arab tribe which has long since perished.

The surrounding land and buildings were sold off piecemeal over the next few years by the Liquidator and a succeeding group of developers. The house itself, with its complement of more than 80 rooms, seemed to represent an insoluble problem in terms of development and planning. Even in the mid-1980s, it was generally regarded as a 'white elephant'. It was eventually put on the market in April 1986 and it passed to a new owner in October of that year. The great question now was whether or not the house would find that stability and continuity of use which it seemed to have been denied over the previous half century.

It must have been quite plain to anyone of realistic

inclination that this Grade A Listed House was extremely unlikely, in the last quarter of the twentieth century, to attract a single owner, in terms of both its restoration costs and general vastness. "Few houses are less adaptable to modern living conditions than a large and uncompromising product of the Greek Revival, and very few are privately inhabited today," is the recently expressed view of one expert.[53] It was also a difficult prospect for a commercial developer to take on as a large number of flats would have had to be created with the resultant problems of changes to the character of the building and the intractibility of the vast public rooms and open spaces. These factors served to cast doubts on the likelihood of obtaining planning permission, especially in the light of previous planning problems over the property.

59 Vandalism in the empty library (1986).

EPILOGUE

The general condition of the House in 1986 was remarkably good. Smirke's original structure was still basically sound with stonework complete and no subsidence. The later stonework, constructed of inferior East Lothian sandstone, principally balustrading erected after 1870, had fared less well and had become extensively eroded. Again, Smirke's windows, made from oak, had survived remarkably well despite many years' absence of any protective coating, whilst later Victorian window frames had rotted. Apart from the roof - of lead with slated sections - which was in need of attention, there was little damage apart from that caused by the succession of occupants.

A J Balfour's historic study had been divided into two by a brick and plaster partition and, somewhat incongruously, a lavatory and bath had been installed. An enormous metal beam had appeared in the magnificent library, a legacy of the days when it was used as school gymnasium. Notice boards ringed the walls of drawing room and music room. Plaster was broken and cracked - the causes ranging from footballs to damp. Hardboard had been nailed to almost all the walls to prevent further deterioration, but when this was removed the original plaster fell away in great slabs. Escape hatches had been knocked through the massive six-foot thick original walls of the House so that young bodies might wriggle through in the event of fire. Central heating pipes had been driven through walls, floors and ceilings with little regard for the aesthetics of the undertaking. Idle young hands had turned to graffiti in the dying days of the school. A locked cupboard on the top floor bore the scrawled words, "Bye, bye Matron," and it was only with a good deal of trepidation that the door was forced open lest it contain some long decayed mortal remains ! The bathrooms and toilets of the school had become a breeding ground for rampant wet rot and dry rot. Woodworm had established a firm hold in the timbers of the roof, and in many of the top floor rooms ingress of water had brought down ceilings.

The only pieces of severe structural damage had, again, been caused by human agency. Burn's arched and balustraded entrance to the side service courtyard (1827) had proved too low for modern pantechnicons to negotiate and had been summarily demolished. Malicious schoolboys had destroyed balustrading at the side of the house, hurling the stonework down the ravine and into the Whittingehame Water. The only remaining occupants, unaffected and unconcerned by all this change and decay, were the long-eared bats who had taken up residence in the absence of human presence.

The magnificent ground floor reception rooms contained virtually all the historically and architecturally significant parts of the house and, fortuitously, the new owner, who had a background of ownership of grand country properties, publisher Charles Skilton from Banwell Castle in the south-west of England, was desirous of keeping all these rooms in use as one single unit for himself. It was proposed then to make five further apartments in other parts of the building: basically, two on the first floor, in nursery and family bedroom accommodation respectively, two on the second floor in the servants' rooms, and one in Burn's 1827 office and domestic extension. The sub-division proposal was logical and did not involve the division of one single room within the House. The smallest apartment was to contain six rooms and others up to 14. But it was, of course, a development which would not have been economic for a commercial developer.

Nevertheless, there were, incredibly, objections to bringing the house back into use in this way on a multiple occupancy basis. One conservationist expressed the view that its character would be better retained if it was allowed to remain as "an elegant ruin": a variation on the somewhat jaundiced view expressed by Marcus Binney in 1974. "Already a large number of houses have been adapted: for educational purposes, as museums and as flats . . . This may preserve their external appearance, but in the vast majority of cases it spells the end of their settings and their contents and brings the introduction of wholly unsympathetic furniture." [54]

However, permission was eventually granted on the basis of the proposed division into six units, which avoided any interference with the principal public rooms on the ground floor (other than their restoration), which ensured their retention as one unit and which provided for no further sub-division at any later date. Outline planning permission was granted on this basis at the end of 1986 with individual owners then being required to obtain Listed Building Consent for proposed works within their own apartments. After more than half a century,

60 Restoration work at the House, 1987.

61 Extensive removal of damaged plaster was required.

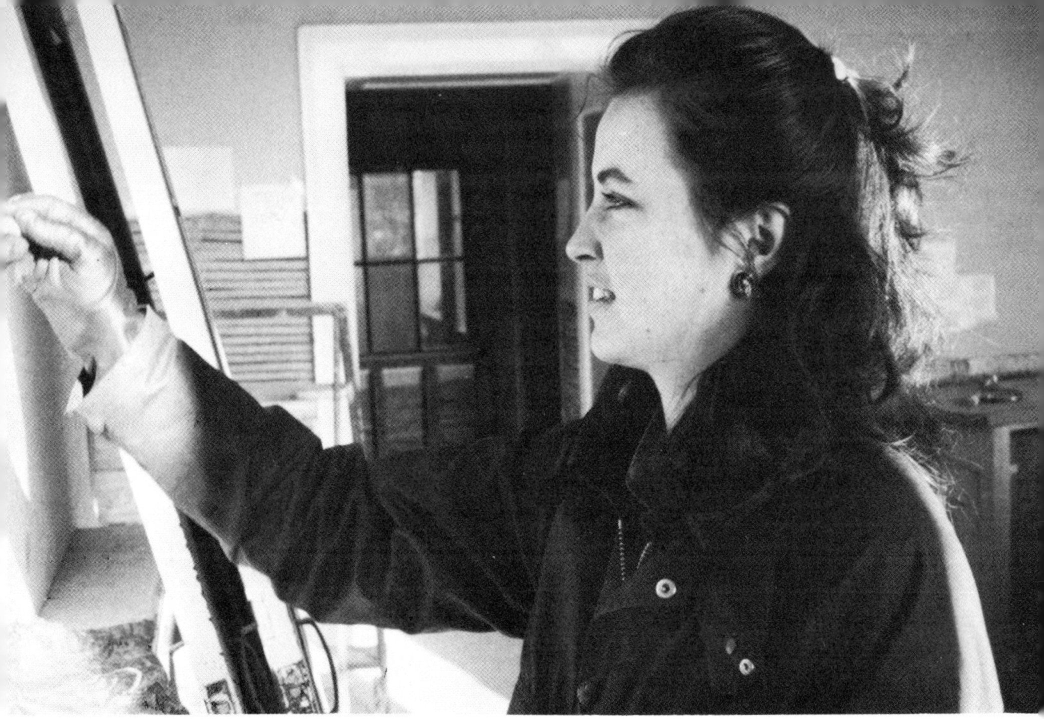

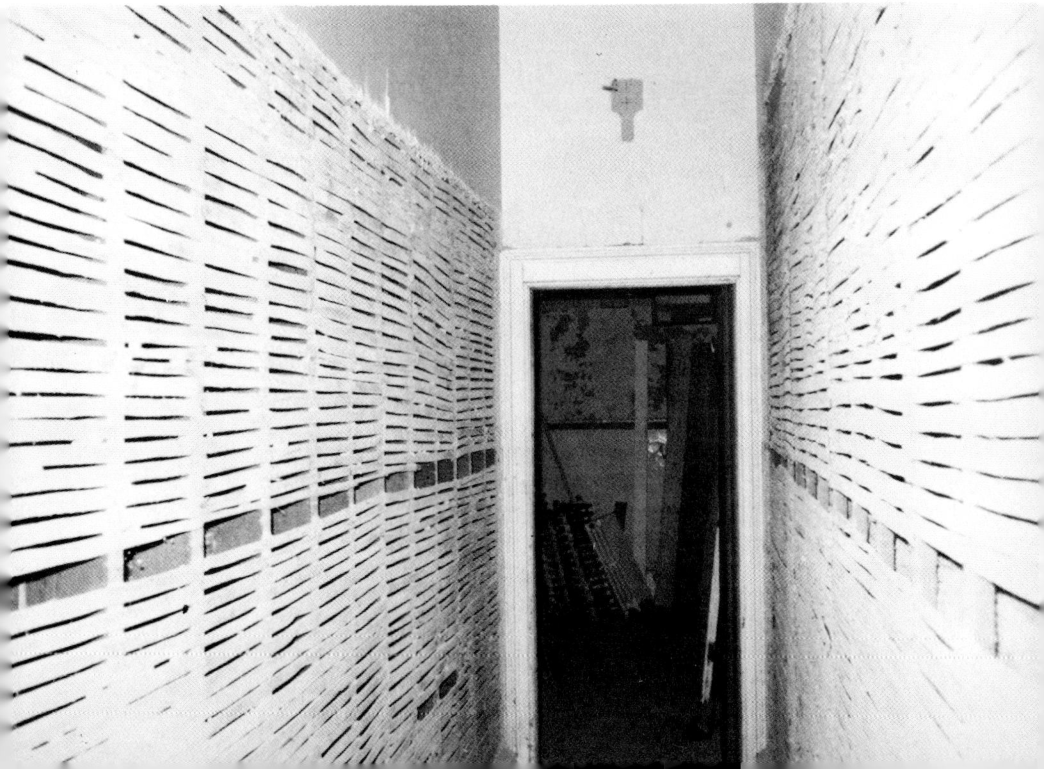

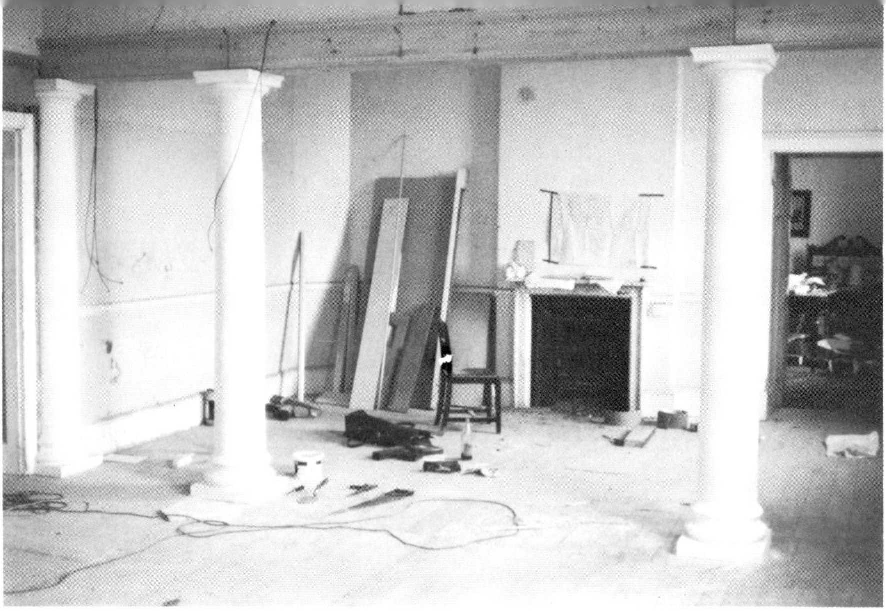

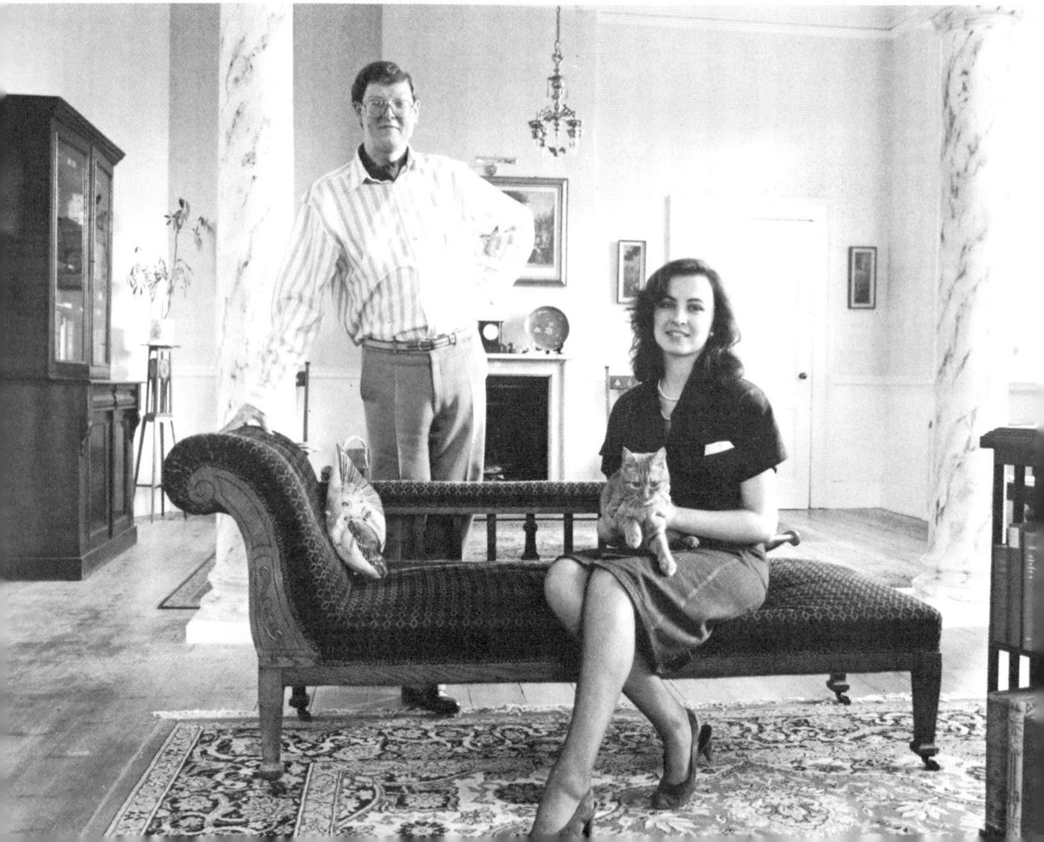

62 New classical pillars in the former nursery, January 1987.

63 Paul & Carol Ann Harris in the same room, May 1989.

the way was open for Whittingehame House to open its doors to residential owners once again.

In many ways, it was a minor miracle that Whittingehame House had survived at all. In 1934, Lord Lothian had been invited to address the annual meeting of the National Trust and he took as his theme, to the general surprise of his audience, the threat to the country house of economic and social pressures. Neither he nor his audience could possibly see ahead to the changes over the horizon. They were possibly dimly aware of the buff envelopes printed OHMS on the hall table, the problems of obtaining - and financing - live-in staff and gardeners, and the ravages of dry rot as regular maintenance became an increasingly expensive item. But multi-ownership, theme parks, schools, health farms and retirement homes were future options of which there was little or no conception at that time. Lothian's prophecy of doom was to be significantly fulfilled. In the 1950s and 60s, before preservation became such a live issue, large and unmanageable country houses were razed to the ground by the hundred and there was widespread official indifference to preservation of the heritage.

Colin McWilliam quotes the Secretary of the Historic Buildings Council for Scotland as observing in 1959 of Sir William Chambers' important masterpiece, Duddingston House, near Edinburgh, "You must admit it's not quite out of the top drawer."[54]. Today, such a remark seems scarcely credible. It is difficult to appreciate just how far private and public attitudes have shifted. For example, it is only since 1968 that it became imperative upon owners to advise the Royal Commission on Ancient Monuments of the demolition of a listed building. Hundreds of buildings in Scotland alone disappeared without the National Monuments Record even having the opportunity to record them photographically - not to mention the more important actual loss to the national heritage. Many other empty properties had simply fell prey to fire, vandals and general deterioration.

In Scotland, between 1875 and 1975, a recorded 318 country houses were destroyed and, of these, 190 disappeared after the Second War.[54] The toll of destruction was severe in East Lothian, especially considering the relatively small size of the county: Belton House (demolished 1967), Caponflat House (1947), Congalton (1927), Elphinstone Tower (1964), Hedderwick Hill (1961), New Hall (1909), Newton Hall (1966), Smeaton Hepburn (1948), Smeaton House (1948) and Thurston (1952). There were especially significant losses at Dunglass House (1950), a bold neo-classical design by Richard Crichton, and Amis-

123

field (1928), Isaac Ware's 18th century masterpiece. Added to this sad list should be many partial demolitions, including that at Biel House.

On the other side of the scale, a number of East Lothian country houses have been successfully converted for multi-occupier use in recent years: Newbyth, Winton, Saltoun and Tyninghame have all, like Whittingehame, been saved by the exercise of this particular option. Fortuitously, Whittingehame had been continuously looked after since 1963 by one caretaker, Allan Cockburn, for whom the preservation of the House had become something of a personal mission, and, before him, there had been James Coleman.

In a curious way, the wheel had come full circle. The House which owed its very existence to a fashion and shift in social circumstances, as James Balfour aspired to the life of a country gentleman, had survived to see a very new type of occupant on the back of a quite different social trend. The country house, spurned for many years as unmanageable and unfashionable, had once again become a desirable and, indeed, much sought after place to live, for a new generation seeking escape from the claustrophobia of modern city life.

James Lees-Milne defines three broad categories of country house: the house created by a great man; the house which became the retreat of a great man; and the house which created a great man.[54] Whittingehame indubitably contributed to the creation of a great man, just as it became his retreat from affairs of state. It is interesting to speculate that something of that indefinable atmosphere might have survived to this day; that that powerful influence of birthplace and residence might in some way be impregnated within the very fabric of the building. It is, of course, mildly ridiculous to credit a building with a personality of its own although we are constantly aware of the differing atmospheres of houses. One has to be fairly insensitive to be unaware of such an apparently illogical and irrational fact. It is, fortunately, not just a simple matter of furniture, silver and pictures. Otherwise, once these are gone, there can be no secure future for any great country house at the end of the 20th century.

Whittingehame, perhaps, goes some way to showing that there can be a future despite many decades of vicissitude.

64 Restoration work in the library. Graffiti and white paint are removed from the scagliola pillars.

65 Door handle designed by Sir Robert Lorimer (1901).

66 Installation of modern plumbing (1986).

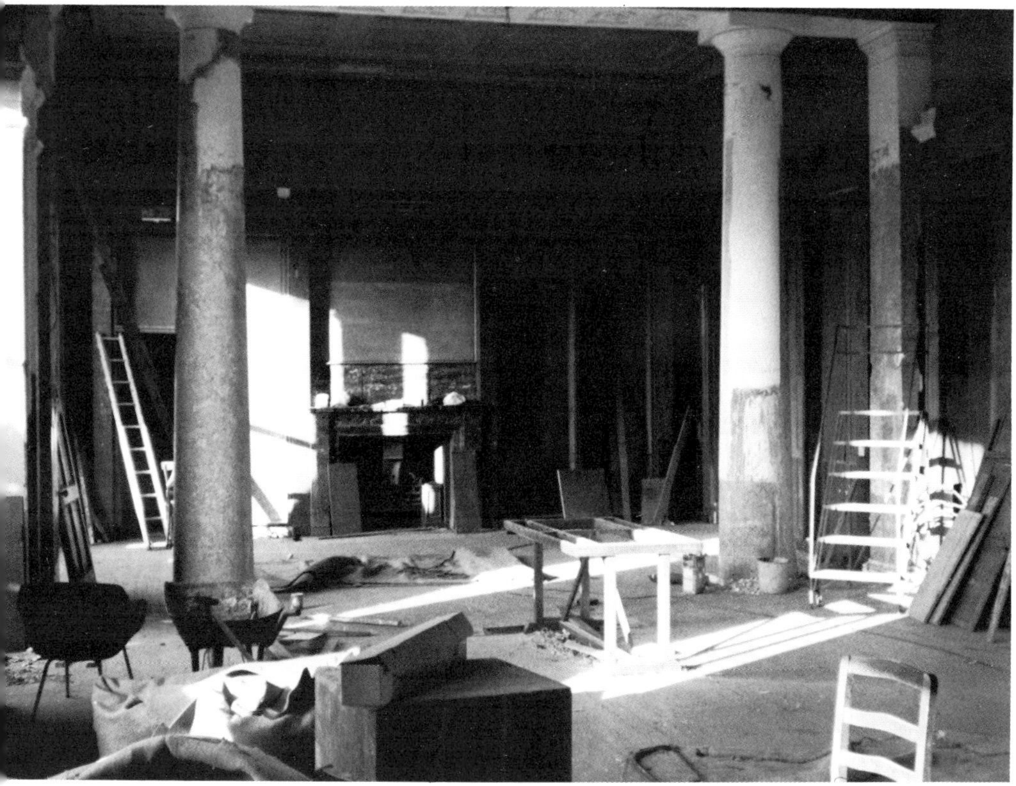

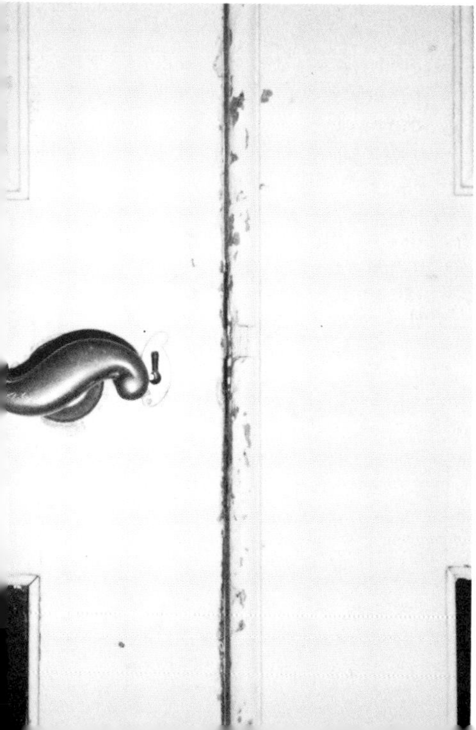

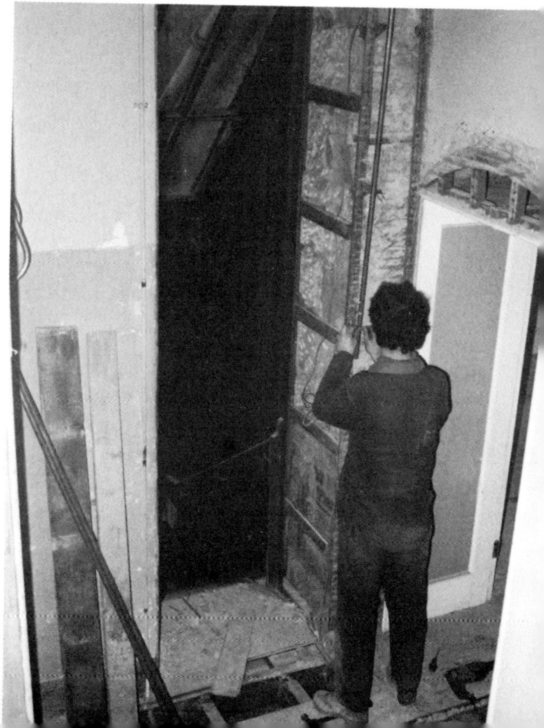

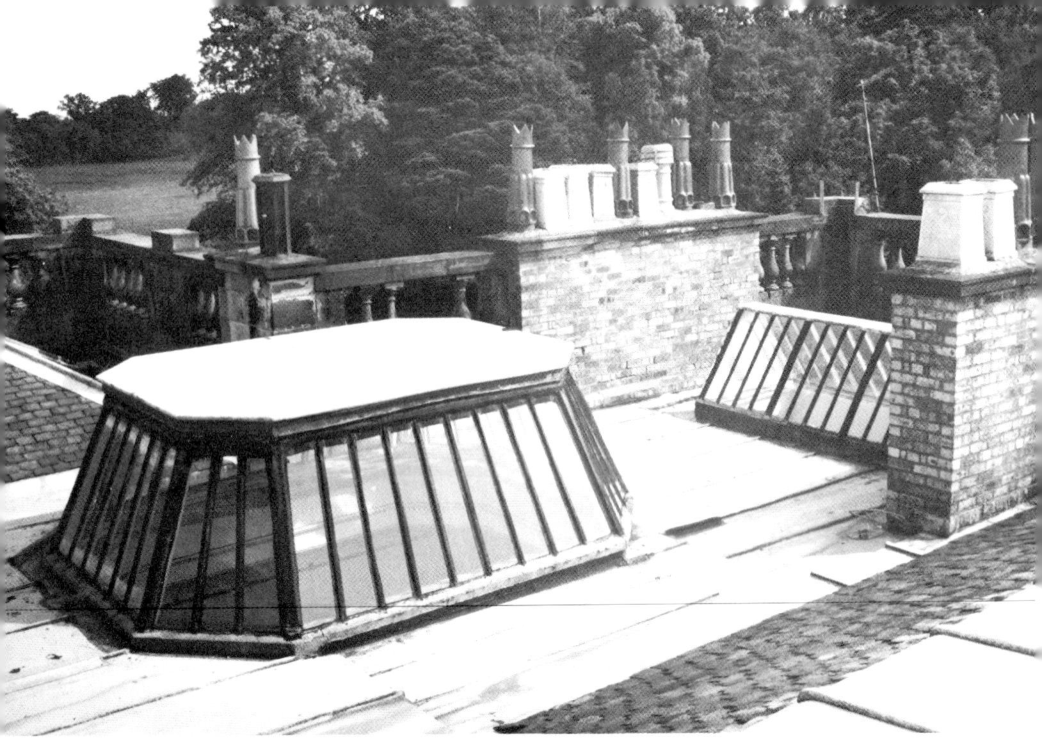

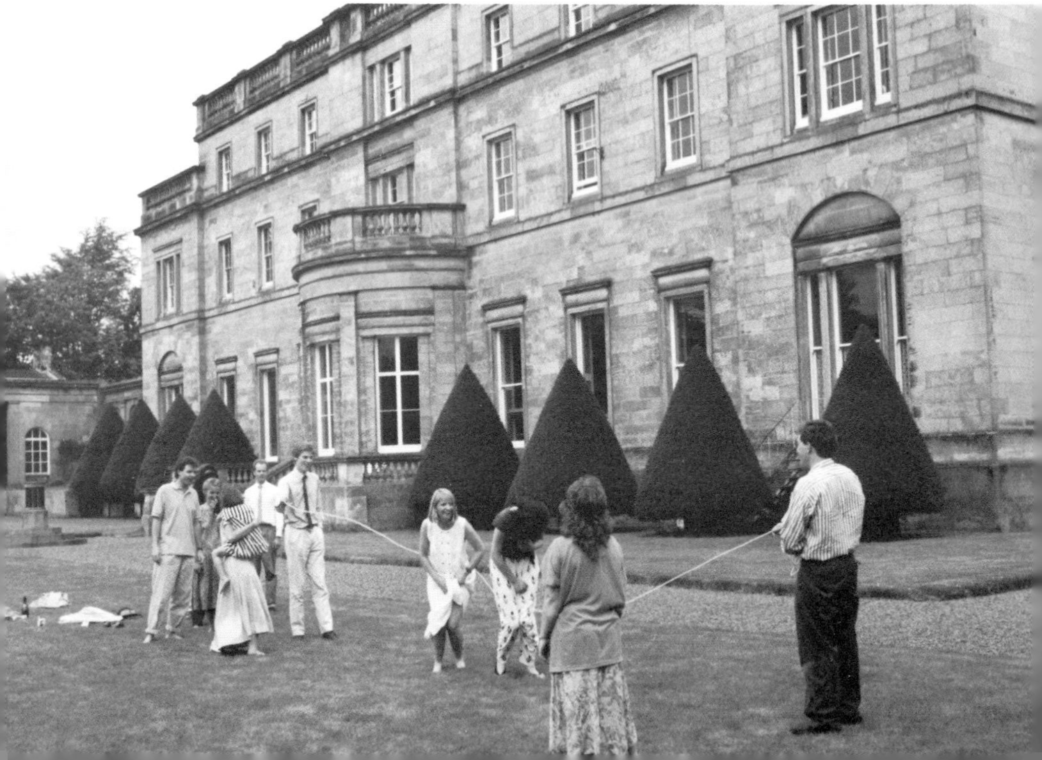

67 The roof of lead with slated sections and two cupolas, over the main stair and the nursery stair.

68 Life returns to the lawns, June 1989.

REFERENCES

Authors and short title. SRO refers to the Balfour Muniment lodged at the Scottish Record Office in Edinburgh. There is a vast amount of material held there and so the source is more precisely identified by the numerical reference under which the letter or document referred to can be found. Full bibliographical information on books and magazines is in the Bibliography.

1 SRO GD433/2/196
2 Lang, Marshall: *Whittingehame*
3 Crook, John Mordaunt: *The Greek Revival*
4 Crook, John Mordaunt: *The British Museum*
5 Small, John: *The Castles and Mansions of the Lothians*
6 Croal, D: *Sketches of East Lothian*
7 Tennant, Margot: *Autobiography*
8 Raymond, E T: *Mr Balfour*
9 McWilliam, Colin: *The Buildings of Scotland*
10 Alderson, Bernard: *Arthur James Balfour*
11 SRO GD433/2/144
12 SRO GD433/2/196: handwritten volume of Balfour history
13 Robertson, Rev. James: *Memoirs of Lady Blanche*
14 SRO GD433/2/97
15 SRO GD433/2/93
16 SRO GD433/2/138
17 SRO GD433/2/215
18 Gladstone, Mary: Diaries & Letters of
19 SRO GD433/2/80: unpublished typescript by Mary Drew/Gladstone
20 Dugdale, Blanche: *Family Homespun*
21 Balfour, Lady Frances: *Ne Obliviscaris*
22 SRO GD433/2/168: Miss Alice Balfour's Entertainments Book
23 SRO GD433/2/M76
24 Webb, Beatrice: *Our Partnership*
25 SRO GD433/2/334
26 Benson, A C: Diaries
27 Dugdale, Blanche: *Arthur James Balfour*
28 SRO GD433/2/306
29 SRO GD433/2/320
30 SRO GD433/2/156
31 SRO GD433/2/140
32 Wodehouse, P G: *Blandings Castle*
33 *The King* magazine
34 SRO GD433/2/502
35 SRO GD433/2/477
36 SRO GD433/2/327
37 SRO GD433/2/388
38 SRO GD433/2/347
39 SRO GD433/2/348
40 SRO GD433/2/251
41 SRO GD433/2/312
42 SRO GD433/2/213
43 SRO GD433/2/372
44 SRO GD433/2/378
45 SRO GD433/2/312

46 SRO GD433/2/383
47 *From Whittingehame 1939 to Israel 1989*
48 Leasor, James: *The Unknown Warrior*
49 Letter from George Rae, Rae & Co. Ltd., to Charles Skilton, August 27 1986
50 *The Phoenix*, The Magazine of Holt School and The Old Jardininan Club, Whittingehame 1974
51 Duncan, Raymond in *The Glasgow Herald*, June 15 1983
52 Letter from P S Williamson for The Secretary of State for Scotland to Ketchen & Stevens W S, April 20 1983
53 Watkin, David: *The Buildings of Britain: Regency*
54 Binney, Marcus & Reid, Peter in *The Destruction of the Country House*

69 Holograph dedication by A J Balfour to Lady Frances Balfour on the flyleaf of *Alfred Lord Tennyson: A Memoir by His Son*, 1899 (ex-Whittingehame House library).

BIBLIOGRAPHY

Books

Abdy, Jane, & Gere, Charlotte: *The Souls*, London 1984
Alderson, Bernard: *Arthur James Balfour*, London 1903
Allen, Nic (Ed.): *Scottish Pioneers of the Greek Revival*, Edinburgh 1984
Asquith, Margot: *The Autobiography of Margot Asquith*, London 1920
Balfour, A J: *Chapters of Autobiography*, London 1930
Balfour, Lady Frances: *Ne Obliviscaris*, London 1930
Benson, A C: *Edwardian Excursions from the Diaries of A C Benson 1898-1904*, ed. by David Newsome, London 1981
Churchill, Winston S: *Great Contemporaries*, London 1937
Collins, Dr. Kenneth: *Aspects of Scottish Jewry*, Glasgow 1987
Croal, D: *Sketches of East Lothian*, Haddington 1873
Crook, John Mordaunt: *The Greek Revival: Neo Classical Attitudes in British Architecture 1760-1870*, London 1972
Crook, John Mordaunt: *The British Museum*, London 1972
Dugdale, Blanche C: *Family Homespun*, London 1940
Dugdale, Blanche C: *Arthur James Balfour*, 2 vols., London 1936
Egremont, Max: *Balfour: A Life of Arthur James Balfour*, London 1980
Girouard, Mark: *Life in the English Country House*, London 1978
Groome, Francis H (Ed.): *Ordnance Gazetteer of Scotland*, London circa 1893
Hannan, Thomas: *Famous Scottish Houses: The Lowlands*, London 1928
Lambourne, Lionel: *The Arts and Crafts Movement: Artists Craftsmen & Designers*, Fine Art Society catalogue, London 1973
Lang, Marshall B: *The Seven Ages of an East Lothian Parish being the Story of Whittingehame from Earliest Times*, Edinburgh 1929
Leasor, James: *The Unknown Warrior*, London 1980
Mackay, Ruddock F: *Balfour: Intellectual Statesman*, Oxford 1985
Martine, John: *Reminiscences and Notices of the Ten Parishes of the County of Haddington*, Haddington 1894
McWilliam, Colin: *The Buildings of Scotland: Lothian*, London 1978
Raymond, E T: *Mr Balfour: A Biography*, London 1920
Robertson, Rev. James: *Lady Blanche Balfour: A Reminiscence*, Edinburgh 1897
Small, John: *The Castles and Mansions of the Lothians*, Edinburgh 1883
Strong, Roy; Binney, Marcus and Harris, John: *The Destruction of the Country House 1875-1975*, London 1975
Tait, A A: *The Landscape Garden in Scotland 1735-1835*, Edinburgh 1980
Watkin, David: *The Buildings of Britain: Regency*, London 1982
Webb, Beatrice: *Our Partnership*, London 1948
Young, Kenneth: *Arthur James Balfour: The Happy Life of the Politician, Prime Minister, Statesman and Philosopher*, London 1963

Newspapers and Journals

Files of *The Scotsman*, *The Glasgow Herald* and *East Lothian Courier*
Article by R A Dakers in *The King* magazine, July 1 1905
Unsigned article (in fact, by Thomas Hannan) in *The Scots Pictorial*, November 15 1919

Old Cast Iron Structures by S B Hamilton in *The Structural Engineer*, London 1949

From Whittingehame 1939 to Israel 1989: 50th Anniversary booklet of the Whittingehame Farm School, Kibbutz Lavie, Israel 1989

Primary Sources

Scottish Record Office, Edinburgh (SRO): Balfour Muniment, under ref. GD433

Plans of William Burn, Royal Commission on the Ancient & Historical Monuments of Scotland, Edinburgh

Plans of Sir Robert Smirke, Royal Institute of British Architects Drawings Collection, London

Dispositions, Register House, Edinburgh

Manuscript material, The British Museum, London

THE EARL OF BALFOUR
Sir Arthur James Balfour, K.G., O.M., and Viscount Traprain, of Whittingehame.

CHRONOLOGY

1773	James Balfour born, Balbirnie, Fife
1812	James Balfour returns to Britain from India
1815	James Balfour marries
1817	Robert Smirke engaged to build Whittingehame House
1820	Birth of James Maitland Balfour
1827	William Burn additions to House
1847	James Balfour dies, James Maitland Balfour inherits
1848	Birth of A J Balfour
1856	Death of James Maitland Balfour
1869	A J Balfour inherits House and estate
1870	Renovations to House and terrace commenced
1874	Death of May Lyttelton
1874	A J Balfour elected M P for Hertford
1886	Secretary for Scotland
1887	Chief Secretary for Ireland
1888	Creation of 7-hole golf course
	Leader of the House of Commons
1899	Remodelling of dining room by Turner
1901	Renovations by Sir Robert Lorimer
1902	King Edward VI visits
1902-5	Prime Minister
1914	Joins the Committee of Imperial Defence
1915	Appointed First Lord of the Admiralty
1916-19	Foreign Secretary
1917	Balfour Declaration drafted at Whittingehame, August
1919-22	Lord President of the Council
1922	Created Earl of Balfour
1925-29	Lord President of the Council
1930	Burial at Whittingehame
1938	Auction sale of contents, October
1939	House turned over to Jewish refugees for farm school
1942	Dr Guthrie's Institution takes over House
1956	Hungarian refugees move in
1963	Holt School for Boys purchases House
1981	Holt School sells House to Mohammed al-Abdaly
1983	Thamoud Ltd liquidated
1986	Purchased by Charles Skilton
1988	House brought back into residential use

GENEALOGY

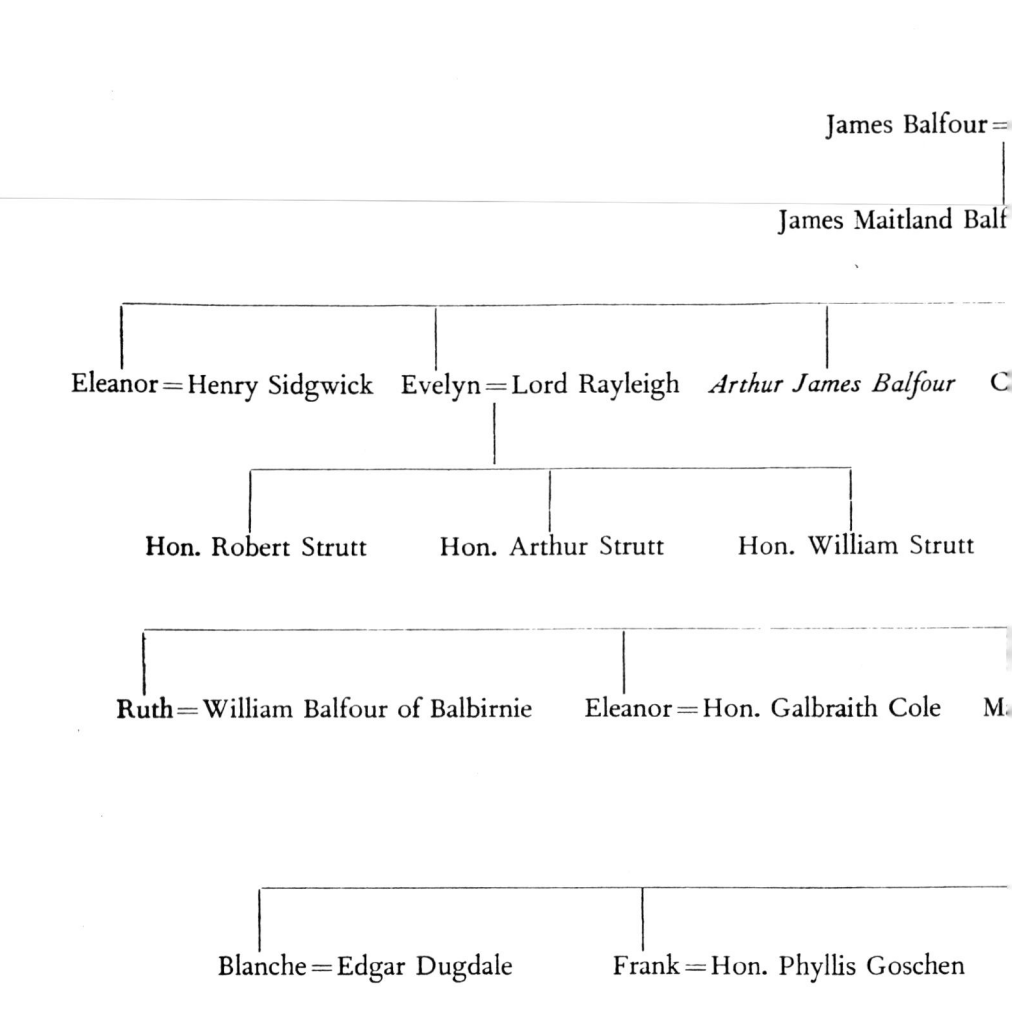

James Balfour =

James Maitland Balf

Eleanor = Henry Sidgwick   Evelyn = Lord Rayleigh   *Arthur James Balfour*   C

Hon. Robert Strutt   Hon. Arthur Strutt   Hon. William Strutt

Ruth = William Balfour of Balbirnie   Eleanor = Hon. Galbraith Cole   M

Blanche = Edgar Dugdale   Frank = Hon. Phyllis Goschen

Eleanor Maitland

Lady Blanche Gascoigne Cecil

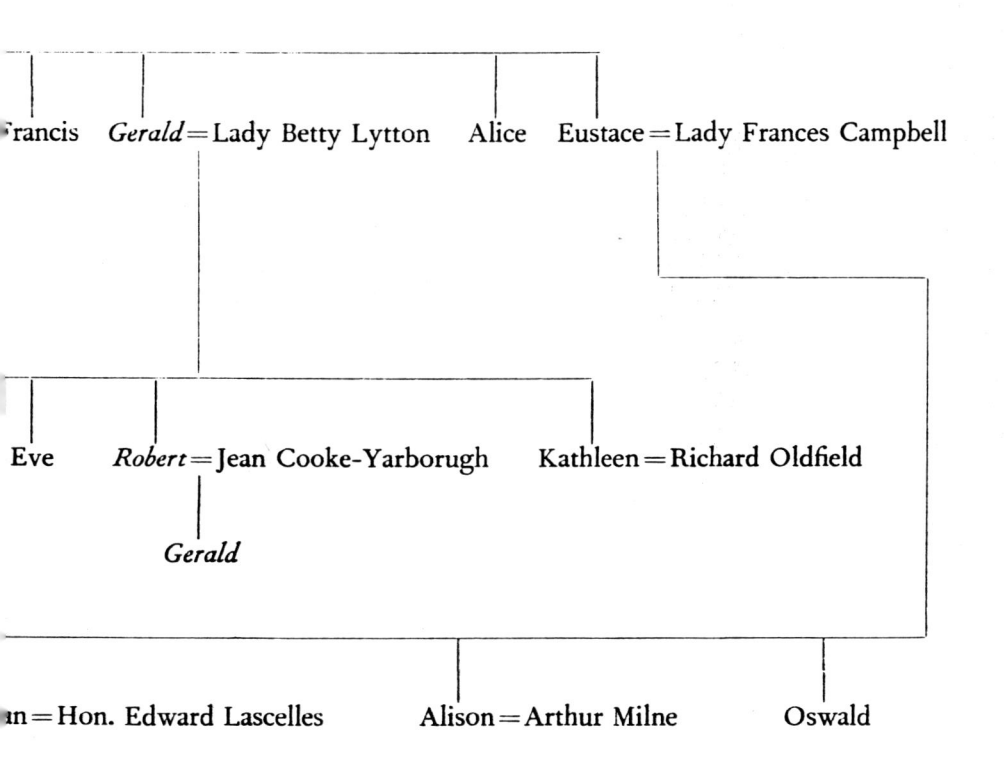

Francis   Gerald=Lady Betty Lytton   Alice   Eustace=Lady Frances Campbell

Eve   Robert=Jean Cooke-Yarborugh   Kathleen=Richard Oldfield

Gerald

an=Hon. Edward Lascelles   Alison=Arthur Milne   Oswald

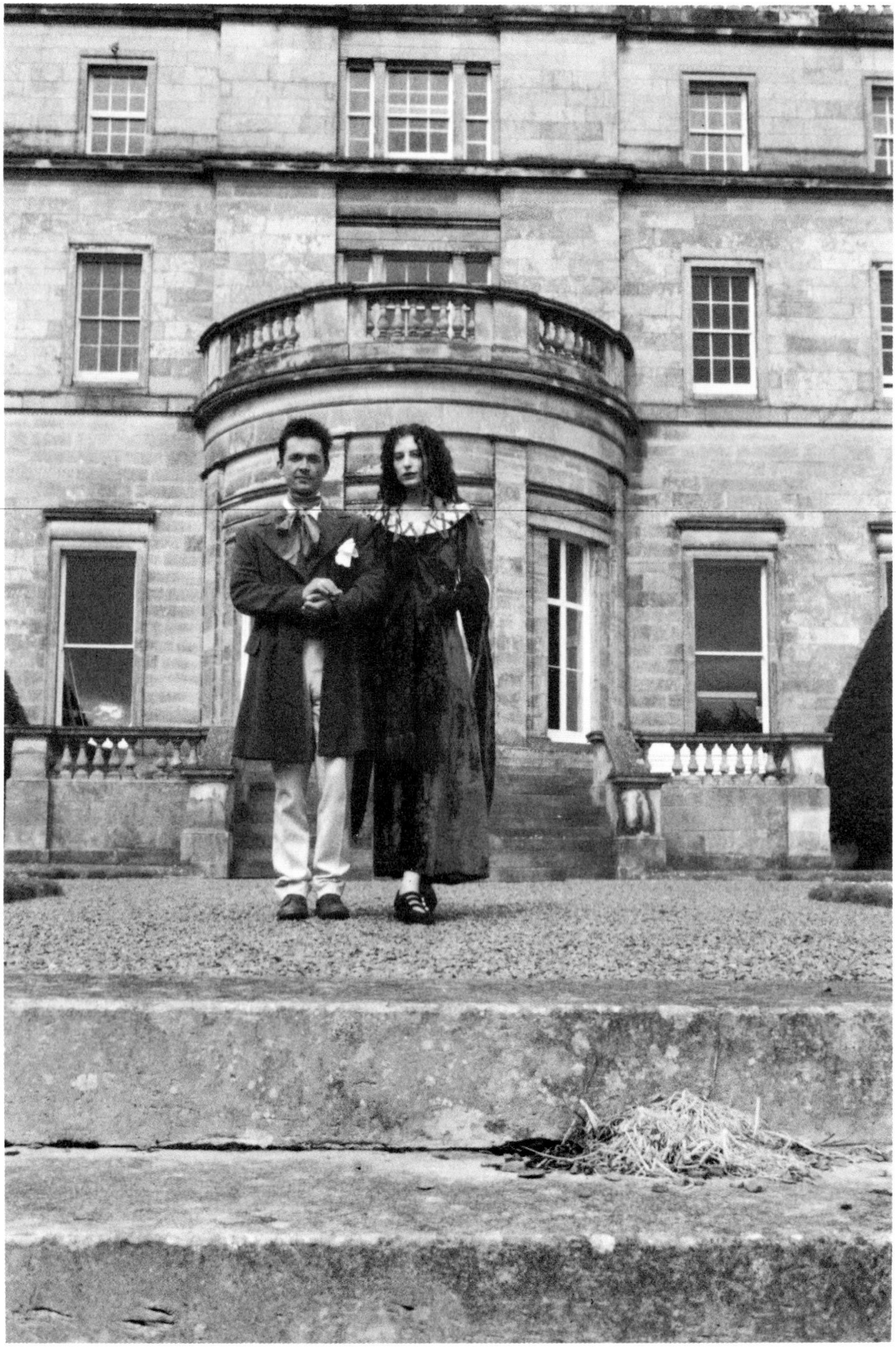

PROPRIETORS OF WHITTINGEHAME HOUSE

June 1989

Charles Skilton Esquire, Hon R W S, F S A (Scot).
Paul Harris Esquire & Mrs Carol Ann Harris
George A S Norman Esquire
Martin Orde Esquire
Alan W Cope Esquire

GLOSSARY OF DOMESTIC & ARCHITECTURAL TERMS

used in the text

Antae, pilasters, the base and capital of which do not conform to the order used elsewhere in the building
Barouche, double-seated four-wheeled carriage with a falling top
Brougham, one horse, closed carriage, named after Lord Brougham (1778-1868)
Buhl cabinets, wooden cabinets with inlaid brass scrolls and other ornamental patterns
Dog-cart, two-wheeled horse-vehicle with seats back to back
Doric, classical Greek forms applied to columns in the building
Freestone, sandstone that cuts well in all directions
Loggia, separate pillared structure
Porte cochere, porch large enough to admit a horsedrawn carriage
Steward's room, office of the most senior member of the household
Still-room, room where drinks like tea, coffee, and toddy were made

70 On the terrace: refugees from the 19th century.

Reproduced by permission of the proprietors of "Punch"

RICKETY

B–L–F–R (Cabinet Maker): "There! It looks lovely!—I only hope it'll hold together!"

(October 7th, 1903)

71 The *Punch* view of the shaky Balfour administration 1902-5.

INDEX

Airlie, Lady Elizabeth, Countess of 29
Alexander of Newmains 21
Alexander of Yarrow 21
Alma Tadema, Sir Lawrence 76
Alvarez, Senorita 105-6
Amery, Leopold 102
Amisfield 124
Anderson, Mrs Helen 66, 68
Arcadius, Emperor 100
Asquith, Lady Cynthia 88
Asquith, Margot (see Tennant, Margot)
Austen, Jane 44

Baker, butler 96, 97
Balbirnie 18
Balfour, Alice 14, 26, 32, 60, 61-2, 77-8, 80-1, 82, 83, 90, 97, 98, 100, 102, 110
Balfour, Ann 39
Balfour, Arthur James
   and books 84-5
   boyhood at Whittingehame 43-50
   burial 109
   cycling 87
   domestic life at Whittingehame 53-4, 60-2, 64-9, 82-5, 90, 95, 104-7
   golf 54, 85-6
   motoring 89-91
   political career 54, 95, 102, 109
   renovations at Whittingehame 71-80, 95, 100
   tennis 87
Balfour, Lady Betty 14, 64, 95, 96, 102
Balfour, Lady Blanche (Lady Blanche Gascoigne Cecil) 39, 43-5, 48, 49-50, 51
Balfour, Blanche, see Dugdale, Blanche
Balfour, Cecil 48, 51, 83
Balfour, Charles 15, 39, 51
Balfour, Lady Eleanor 16, 26, 29-30, 39
Balfour, Eustace 13, 46, 71-2, 74, 75, 76, 98
Balfour, Lady Eve 66, 104
Balfour, Evelyn 42, 83
Balfour, Lady Frances 13, 64-6, 69, 76, 81, 82, 86, 89, 90, 95-6, 97, 102, 104, 105, 109
Balfour, Francis 51
Balfour, Gerald 14, 83, 98, 109
Balfour, James, of Balbirnie 15-17, 26, 29, 34
Balfour, James Maitland 39, 42
Balfour, John 39
Balfour, Mary 39
Balfour, Nora 83
Balfour, Oswald 95, 96, 97, 98
Balfour Declaration, The 102-3
Balgonie 16, 39

Beatty, Admiral Sir David 98
Beaverbrook, Lord 99
Belton House 123
Benson, A C 14, 59, 64, 69
Biel House 76, 124
Birkenhead, Lord 63
British Museum 17, 26
Brocks, pyrotechnists 61
Buckingham Palace 19
Burn, William 23, 34-8, 120
Burne-Jones, Edward 75, 110
Burne-Jones, Philip 75
Buxton, Sir Thomas 89

Caponflat House 123
Carlton Gardens 51, 96, 100
Cassells, publishers 104
Cecil, Lady Blanche (see Balfour, Lady Blanche)
Chamberlain, Joseph 59
Churchill, Winston S 59, 95, 103-4
Cockburn, Allan 124
Coleman, James 109, 110, 124
Conan Doyle, Sir Arthur 59, 84
Congalton Hall 123
Cook-Yarborough, Jean 102, 110
Covent Garden Theatre 17
Crichton, Richard 124
Cullels Quarry 21
Curzon, Lord (George) 58

Dakers, R A 84
Dawson, Lord 104
Desborough, Lady (Etty) 58, 59
Dorward, James 21
Dowells, auctioneers 110
Drew, Mary (see Gladstone, Mary)
Duddingston House 123
Duffield, Margaret 50
Dugdale, Blanche (Mrs Edgar Dugdale) 13, 14, 58, 64, 66-9, 84, 89, 97, 104, 105, 110
Dunglass House 124

Eastnor Castle 17
East Linton 78, 89, 96, 97, 104
Edward VII, His Majesty King 63, 90
Elcho, Cynthia (see Asquith, Lady Cynthia)
Elcho, Lady 54, 59, 98
Elcho, Lord 58
Eliot, Sir Charles 89
Ellis, Walter Scott 112
Ellis, William Shakespeare 112
Elphinstone Tower 123

Faithfull, Miss Emily 44
Farquharson, of Haddington 71
Fisher, Alexander 72-4
Foundations of Belief, The 27

George V, His Majesty King 61
Gilpin, Captain J B 30
Gilpin, W S 30

138

Gladstone, Mary 53-6, 82-3
Gladstone, W E 53, 59
Gosford House 88, 98
Gower, Captain Leveson 97
Guthrie's, Dr, Institution for Boys 112

Haddington, Earl of 48
Hagley Hall 52-3
Half Moon Lodge 32
Hamilton, J Nisbet 48
Hatfield House 51, 54
Hawarden 54
Hay, William 16
Hedderwick Hill 123
Hedley Smith, factor 102
Henshaws, architectural ironmongers 76
Hill, Oliver 75
Holt School for Boys 113-16
Hope, Henry 48
Horne, Sir Robert 63
Hunter, Lord 112

Innes, T Mitchell 48
Inverary Castle 81

Jewish refugees - at Whittingehame 110-12
Joshua, Mrs 102-3

Kahn, Mrs O 102-3
Keats, John 85
Kennedy, G R M & Partners 117
Kinfauns Castle 17, 30
Kinloch, Alexander 48
Kinmount 17, 34
Kipling, Rudyard 85
Kitchener, Admiral Lord 63
Kling, Misses Amalie and Auguste 44, 48

Law, Andrew Bonar 59, 63
Linton (see East Linton)
Lloyd George, David 59, 63
Lorimer, Sir Robert 76, 125
Lowther Castle 17
Luton Hoo 17
Lyttelton, Lavinia 53, 82
Lyttelton, May 53
Lyttelton, Spencer 52-3

Malcolm, Ian 105
Mills, chauffeur 89, 91, 104
Mohammed al-Abdaly 116
Morgan, William De 75
Morris, William 75

Newbyth 124
New Hall 123
Newton Don 17
Newton Hall 123
Nomburg, Harry 112
Normanby Hall 17
North Berwick 86
Nunraw 88

Oak Inn 116
Overfield 87

Peco 98
Pressmennan Lake 33

Rayleigh, Lord 83
Read, Lawrence 116
Redcliff 110
Rintoul, William 79
Robertson, Reverend James 14, 39, 49-50, 97
Rosyth 98

Salisbury, Lord 51, 54, 59, 95
Saltoun Hall 124
Scarborough 97
Scott, Reverend Walter 49
Sibbalds of Edinburgh 76
Sidgwick, Henry 83
Simpson, Sir James 45
Skilton, Charles 11, 120
Smeaton Hepburn 123
Smeaton House 123
Smirke, Sir Robert 17-23, 34, 38, 39, 119
Solomon, Captain Robert 110
Souls, The 53-5, 58, 60
Speculative Society, The 82
Stevenson, Robert Louis 85
Strathconan 16, 54

Talbot, Edward 82
Tennant, Laura 55, 58
Tennant, Margot 21
Thamoud Ltd 117
Thurston 123
Traprain Law 100-1
Turner, Lawrence 71-2
Tyninghame 124

Victoria, Her Majesty Queen, Diamond Jubilee Celebrations for 61-3

Ware, Isaac 124
Webb, Beatrice 14, 59, 63-4, 81-2
Wedderburn, Dr 96, 97, 104
Weizmann, Chaim 109
Wells, H G 59
Wemyss, Lord 98
Wet Carbonising 98
Whitekirk 95-6
Whittinghame Advertiser 45-8
Whittingehame, village of 33-4
    Church 34, 63, 109
    Farm School 110-12
    Home Farm 61
    Tower 30, 32-3
Winton House 32, 124
Wodehouse, P G 81

Yester 98
Younger, George 117

APPENDIX I

BALFOUR, 1st Earl of, *cr.* 1922, and Viscount Traprain of Whittingehame; **Arthur James Balfour,** K.G. 1922; P.C., F.R.S., O.M. 1916; D.L. East Lothian; Chancellor of Edinburgh University; Chancellor of Cambridge University, 1919; Elder Brother of Trinity House; President of the Council, 1919-22 and since 1925; *b.* Scotland, 25 July 1848; *e. s.* of late James Maitland Balfour, Whittingehame, Haddingtonshire (*d.* 1856), and Lady Blanche Gascoigne Cecil, 2nd *d.,* of 2nd Marquis of Salisbury; unmarried. *Educ.:* Eton; Trin. Coll. Camb. (M.A.). Hon. LL.D. Edin., 1881; St. Andrews, 1885; Camb., 1888; Dublin and Glasgow, 1891; Manchester, 1908; Liverpool, 1909; Birmingham, 1909; Bristol, 1912; Sheffield, 1912; Columbia, 1917; Hon. D.C.L. Oxon, 1891; Litt. D. University of Wales, 1921; Ph. D. University of Cracow, 1923; LL.D. Athens, 1924; LL.D. Leeds, 1924; M.P. (C.) for Hertford, 1874-85; acted for a time with "Fourth Party"; Private Secretary to Marquis of Salisbury when Secretary of State for Foreign Affairs, 1878-80; employed on Special Mission of Lords Salisbury and Beaconsfield to Berlin, 1878; Privy Councillor, 1885; President of Local Government Board, 1885-86; Secretary for Scotland with seat in Cabinet; Vice-President of Committee of Council on Education for Scotland, 1886-87; Lord Rector, St. Andrews University, 1886; Chief Secretary for Ireland, 1887-91; Member of Gold and Silver Commission, 1887-88; elected Member of Senate, London University, 1887; F.R.S. 1888; Lord Rector, Glasgow University, 1890; created Congested Districts Board for Ireland, 1890; Member l'Académie des Sciences morales et politiques (L'Institut de France); Leader House of Commons and First Lord of Treasury, 1891-92; Leader of Opposition, 1892-95; President British Association, 1904; Prime Minister, 1902-5; 1st Lord of Treasury and Leader of House of Commons 1895-1906; M.P. Eastern Division of Manchester, 1885-1906; Gifford Lecturer, Glasgow University, 1913-14 and 1922-23; First Lord of the Admiralty, 1915-16; Foreign Secretary, 1916-19; M.P. (C.U.) City of London, 1906-22; Head of British Mission to America, 1917; British Mission to Washington Conference, 1921-22; President British Academy, 1921-28. *Publications:* A Defence of Philosophic Doubt, 1879; Essays and Addresses, 1893 (third and enlarged edition, 1905); The Foundations of Belief, being Notes introductory to the Study of Theology, 1895 (cheap edition, 1901); Economic Notes on Insular Free Trade, 1903; Reflections Suggested by the New Theory of Matter, 1904; Speeches (1880-1905) on Fiscal Reform, 1906; Criticism and Beauty (Romanes Lecture), 1909; Theism and Humanism (Gifford Lectures, 1914), 1915; Essays, Speculative and Political, 1920; Theism and Thought, 1923; Opinions and Argument, 1927. *Recreations:* motoring, tennis. *Heir: b.* Rt. Hon. Gerald William Balfour, *q. v. Address:* 4 Carlton Gardens, S.W.1; Whittingehame, Prestonkirk, East Lothian. *Clubs:* Carlton, Travellers', Athenæum; New, Edinburgh.

Entry for Arthur James Balfour, 1st Earl of Balfour, from *Who's Who* (1929).

APPENDIX II

Whittingehame Clothing Society.

RULES AND ARRANGEMENTS.

I. The object of the Society is to assist families and individuals in providing useful clothing at less than usual cost, which is effected by interest paid by Miss Balfour on the members' subscriptions, and by a reduction the tradesmen employed are enabled to make, owing to the ready-money payment, and to the quantity bought.

II. Any married woman, and any widow, unmarried woman, or girl who is earning money may become a member of the Society, provided they either reside in the parish of Whittingehame, or they or their husbands work for Mr Balfour.

III. Members can only join the Society in November or May.

IV. Miss Balfour, or others appointed by her, will receive subscriptions from members monthly, on appointed days, in sums of not less than 6d. a month.

V. Members who have subscribed REGULARLY will have *twopence* interest added by Miss Balfour to every *shilling* paid in by them, and will then receive the whole amount in articles of clothing.

VI. *Subscriptions which are not paid every month regularly will be returned* to the member *without addition* made to them. The same will be done in case of a member leaving the parish, or not wishing to continue in the Society. In case of death the subscriptions will be returned to the nearest relatives.

VII. About the beginning of November each member will receive an order, to the amount of her subscription with interest. She can then select any of the goods named in Rule X. to the value of her order.

VIII. The following tradespeople will supply goods to the members of the Whittingehame Clothing Society :—*Messrs KELLIE, Haddington; Messrs WILLIAMSON & SPARK, Haddington; Mr MAIN, Haddington; Misses KNOX, East Linton; Mr ANDREW WATT, East Linton.* On giving up their Cards at the end of the year Members should state on which tradespeople they wish to have their order made out.

IX. ....
has kindly consented to receive subscriptions from Members residing at ....
The collecting days are .... and every ....
four weeks after.

X. The Goods which will be supplied to Members of the Whittingehame Clothing Society will consist of all useful materials and articles of dress, blankets, sheetings, and other materials for household use, but NOT things that are only for ornament, such as silk articles, feathers, artificial flowers, etc.

The Rules of the Whittingehame Clothing Society, founded at the instigation of Alice Balfour.

72 Whittingehame House from the south west, 1987.